)uet Treasures

olume 1 • Beginning

THE F·J·H MUSIC COMPANY INC.
Frank J. Hackinson

Production: Frank J. Hackinson
Production Coordinators: Joyce Loke and Satish Bhakta
Cover Design: Terpstra Design, San Francisco, CA
Cover Art Concept: Helen Marlais
Cover Illustration: Marcia Donley
Engraving: Tempo Music Press, Inc.
Printer: Tempo Music Press, Inc.

ISBN 1-56939-722-8

About the Series

Duet Treasures Volume 1 and Volume 2 are devoted to wonderful duet repertoire for the adult piano student. The fine composers and arrangers in this series were commissioned to create engaging original duets as well as arrangements of famous pieces. This series complements other FJH publications, and is artistically strong, carefully leveled, and pedagogically sound. Have fun enjoying this wonderful collection of duets!

Table of Contents

Ode to Joy

Theme from *Symphony No. 9*

Secondo

Ludwig van Beethoven
arr. Timothy Brown

With much joy (♩= ca. 152)

Play both hands one octave lower throughout

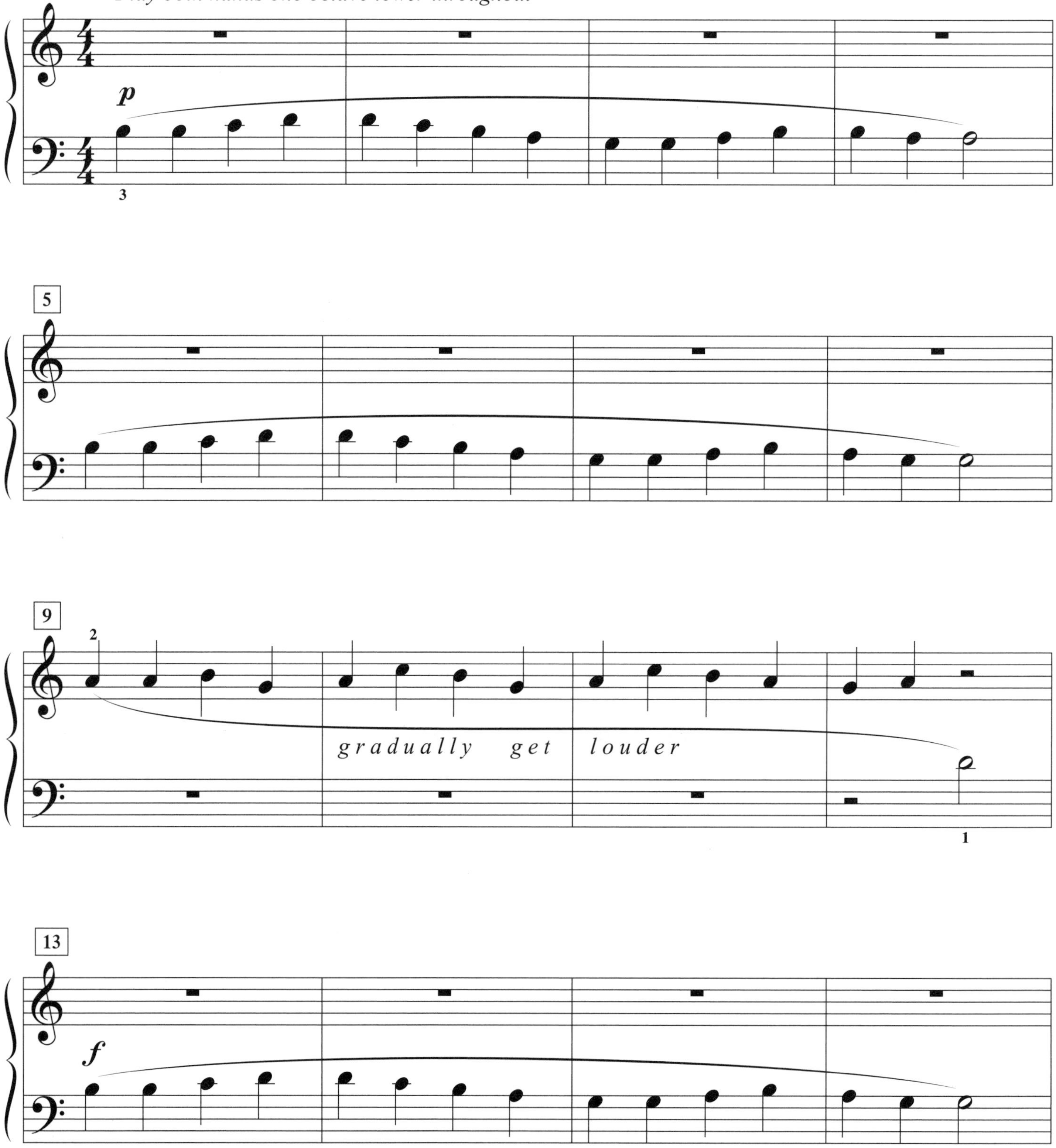

Ode to Joy

Theme from *Symphony No. 9*

Primo

Ludwig van Beethoven
arr. Timothy Brown

With much joy (♩= ca. 152)

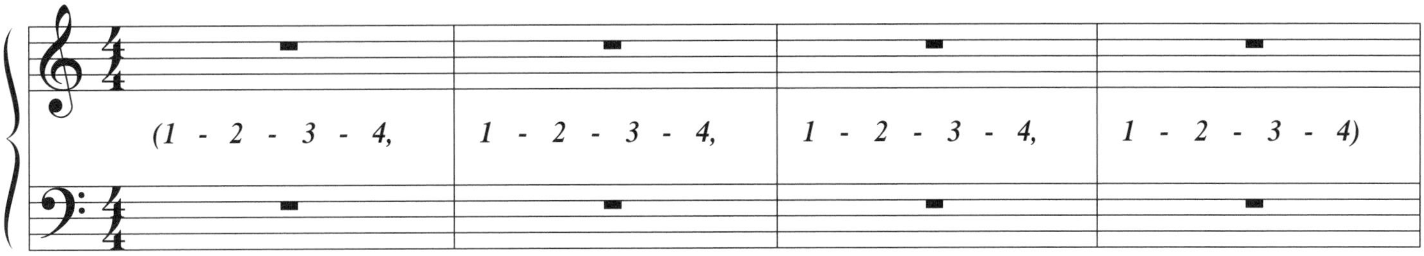

5 *Play both hands one octave higher throughout*

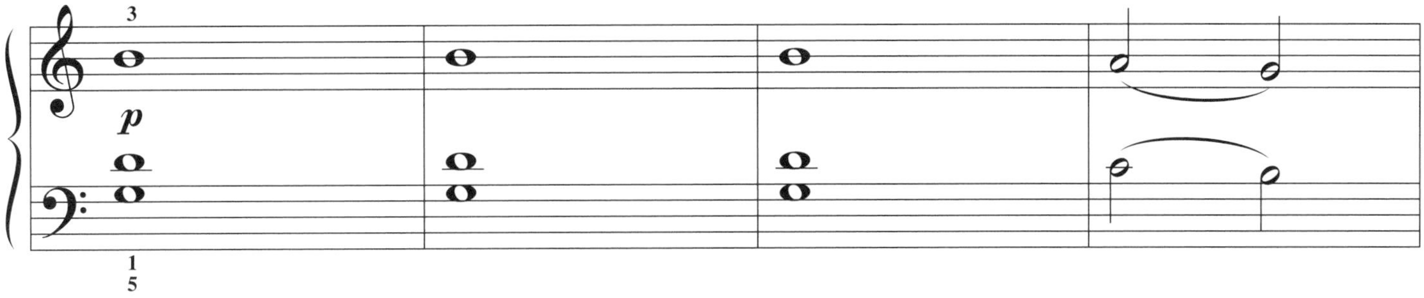

9

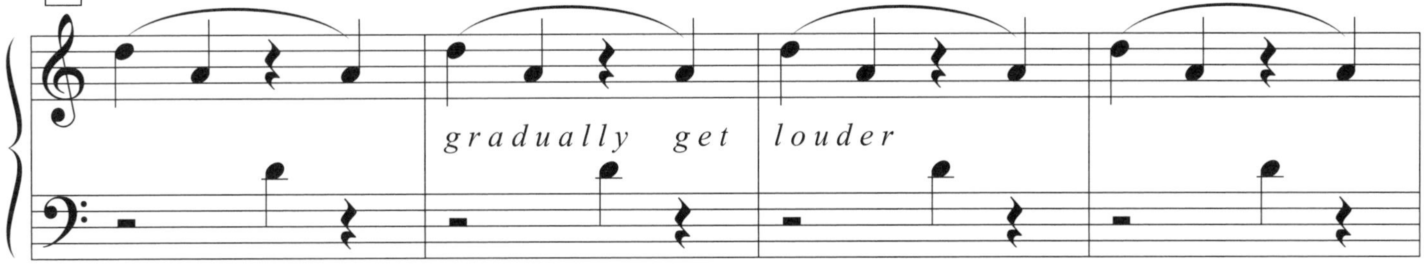

13

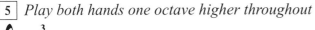

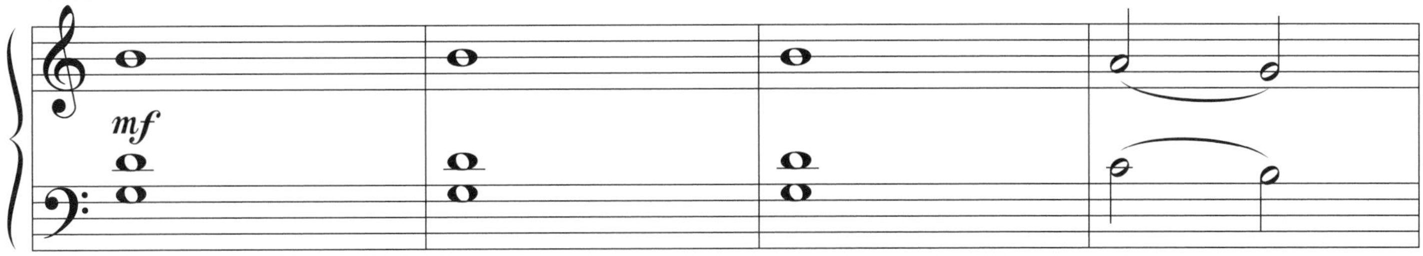

Secondo

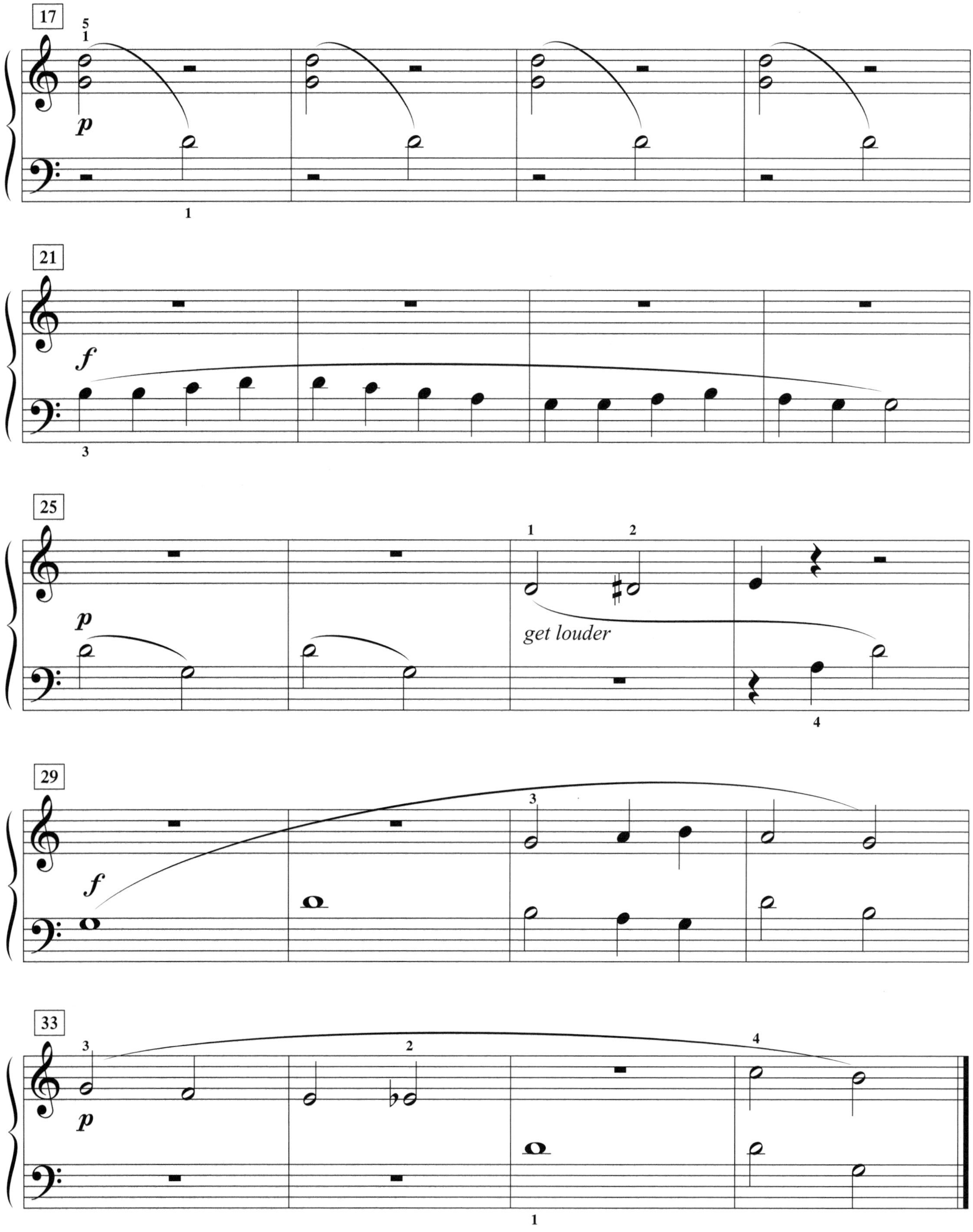
17
p
21
f
25
p
get louder
29
f
33
p

Primo

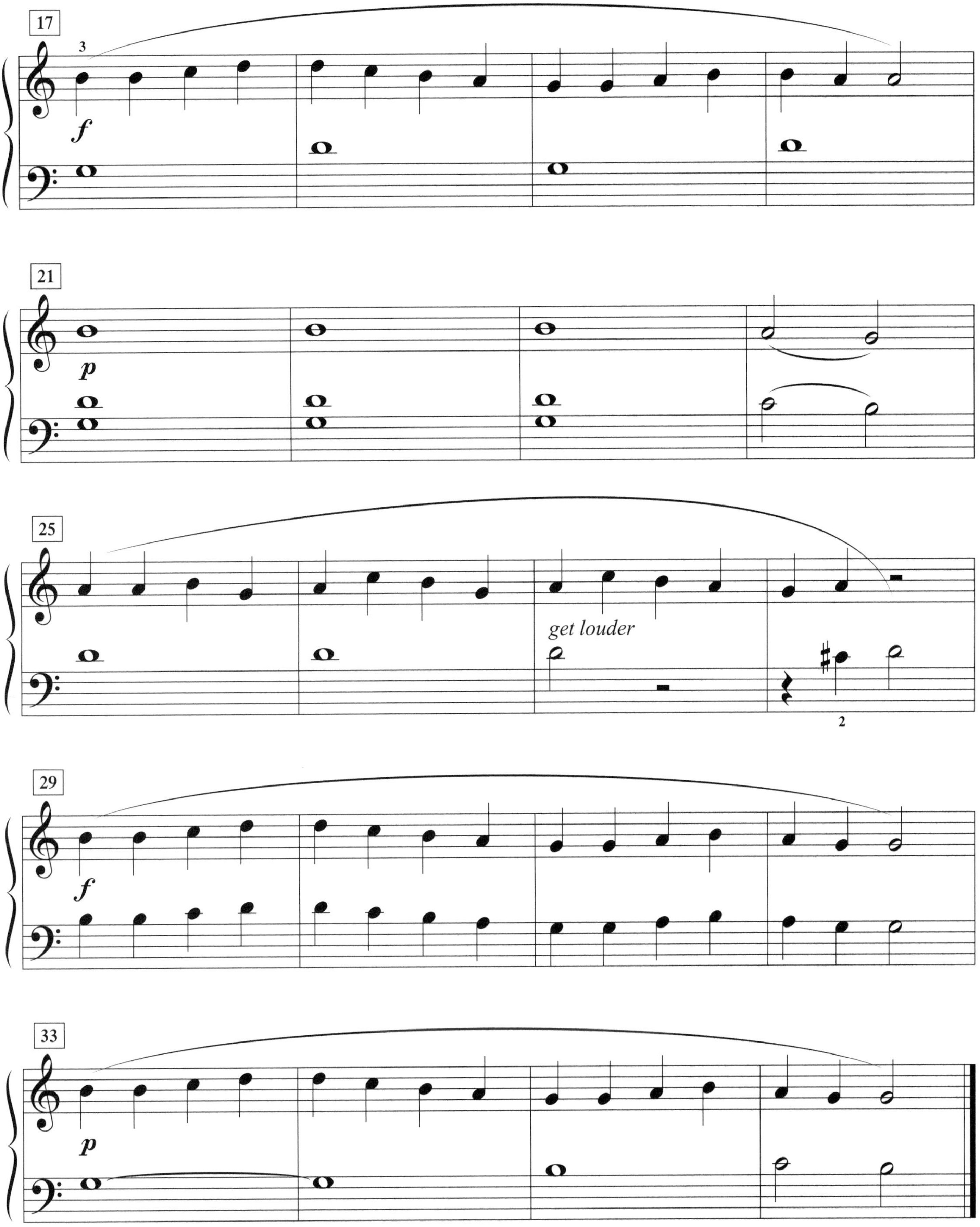

Take Me Out to the Ball Game

Secondo

Words: Jack Norworth
Music: Albert von Tilzer
arr. Edwin McLean

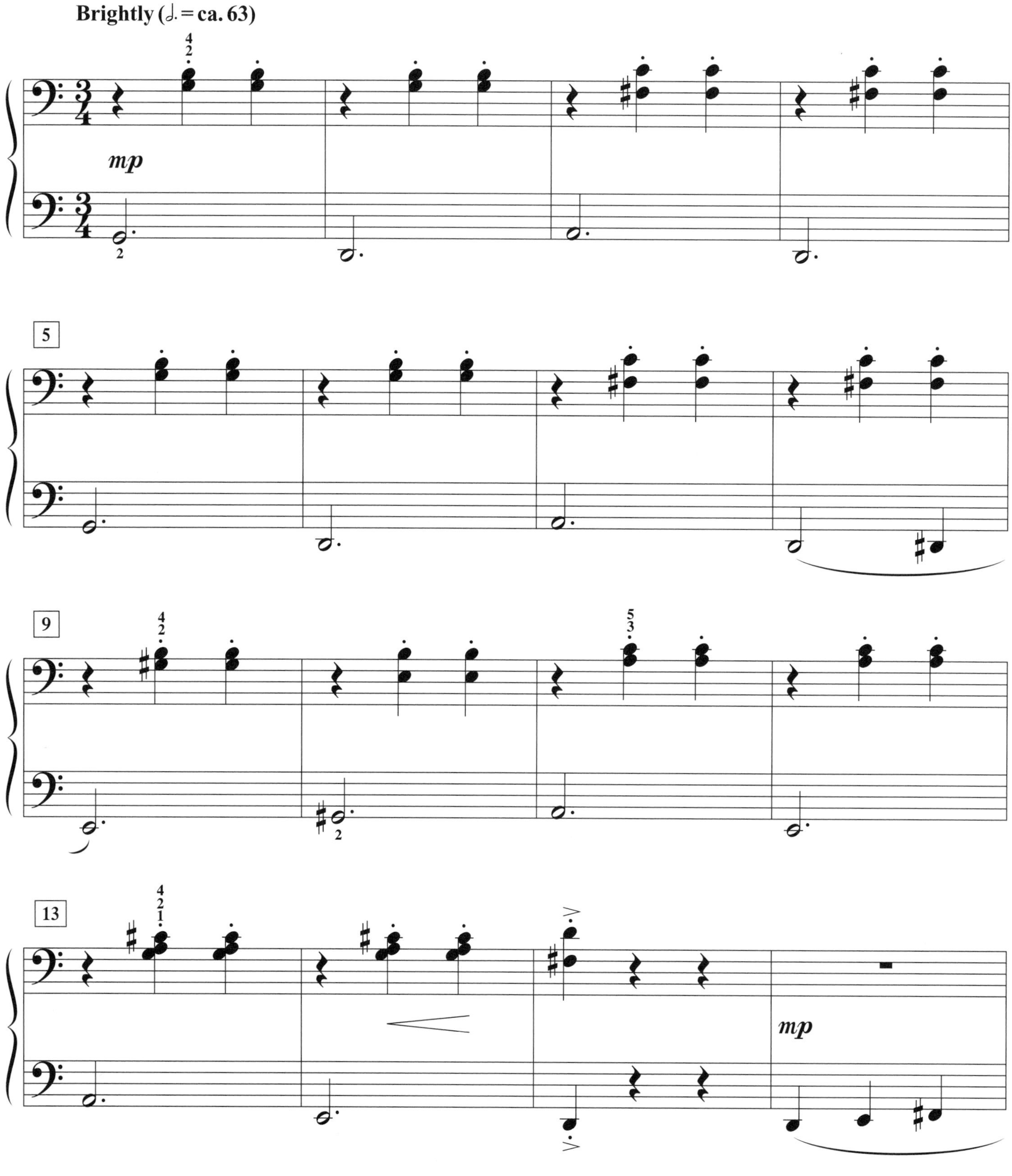

Take Me Out to the Ball Game

Primo

Words: Jack Norworth
Music: Albert von Tilzer
arr. Edwin McLean

Brightly (♩. = ca. 63)
Play both hands one octave higher throughout

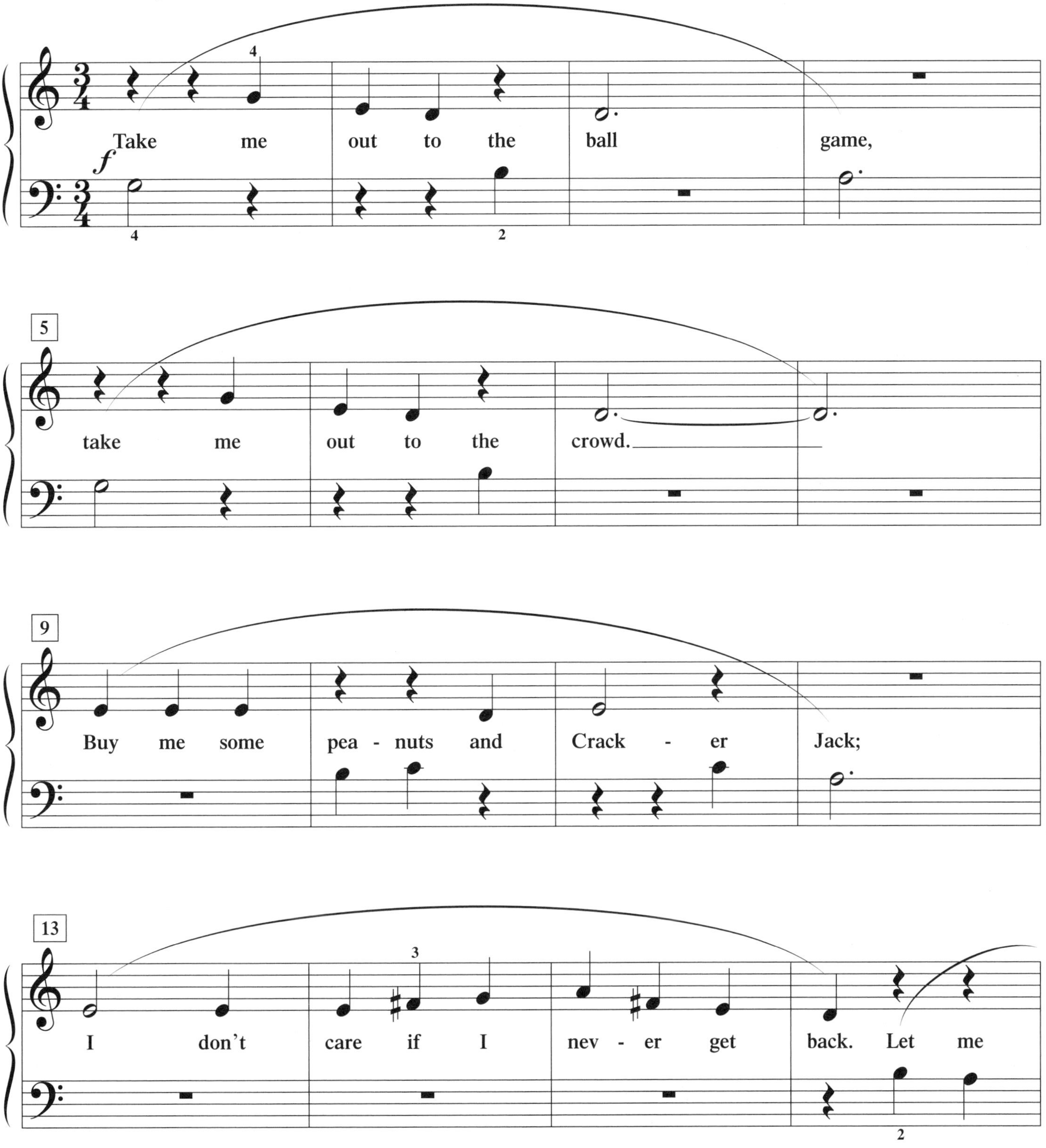
f
Take me out to the ball game,
5
take me out to the crowd.
9
Buy me some pea - nuts and Crack - er Jack;
13
I don't care if I nev - er get back. Let me

Secondo

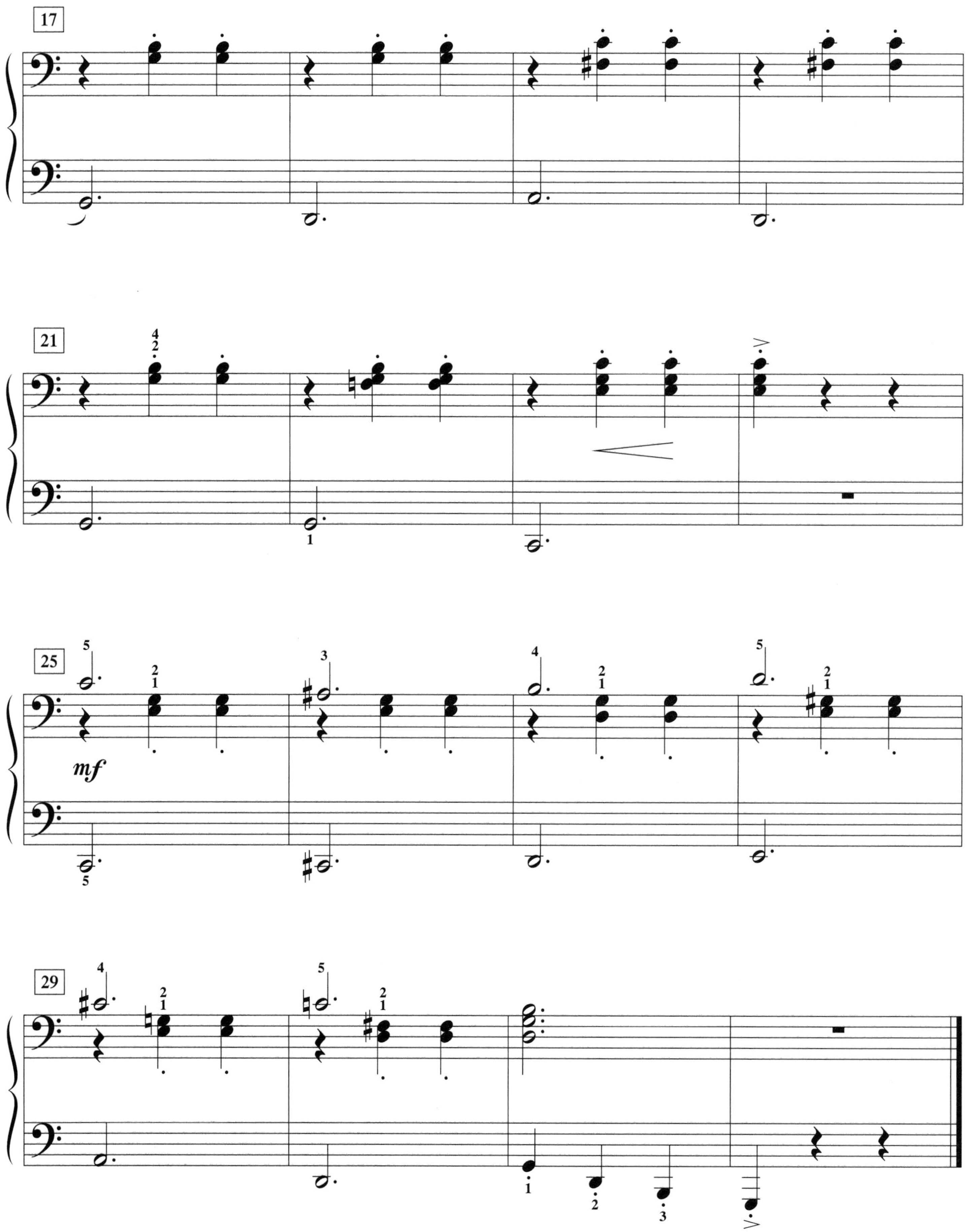

Primo

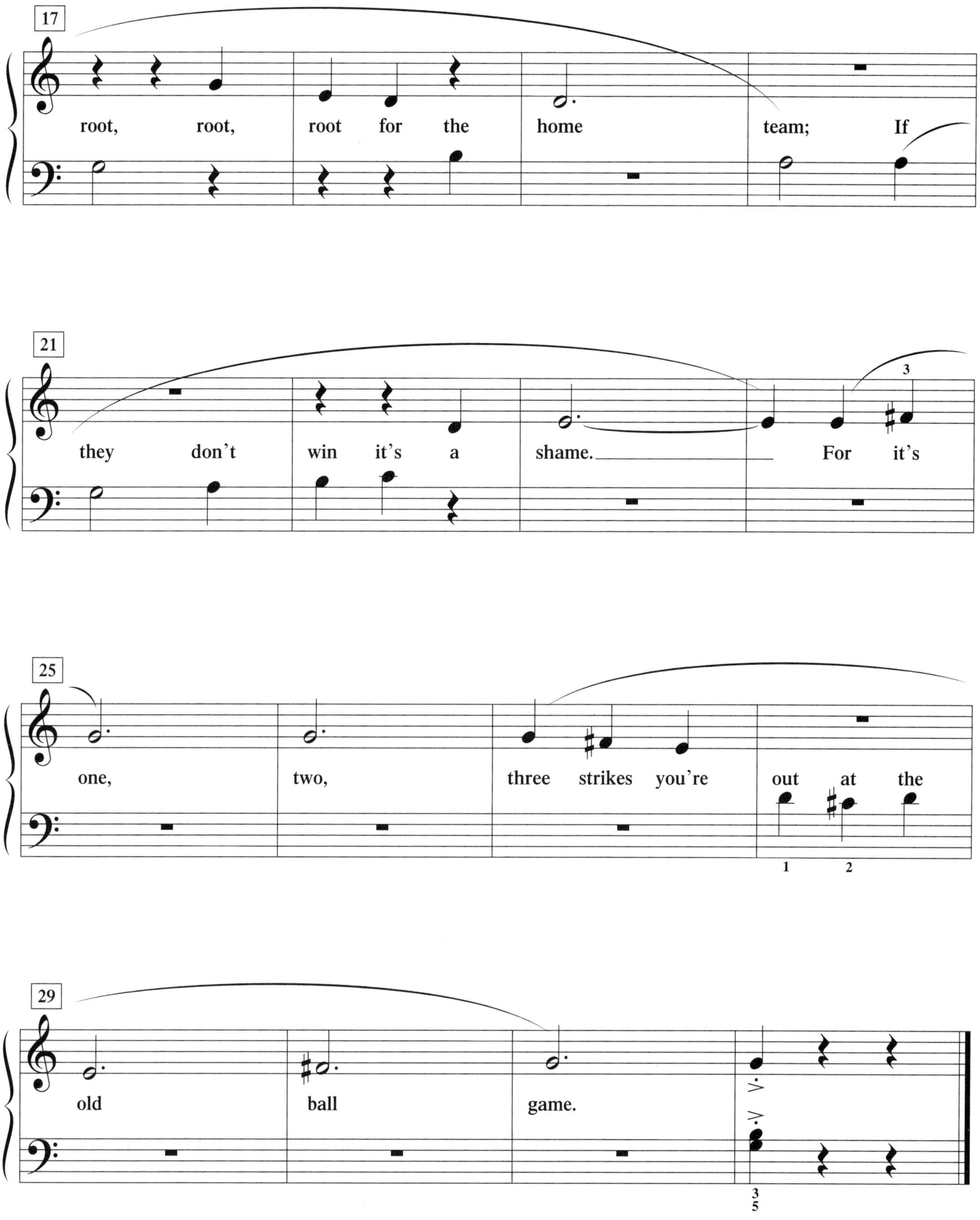
17
root, root, root for the home team; If
21
they don't win it's a shame. For it's
3
25
one, two, three strikes you're out at the
1 2
29
old ball game.
3
5

Hymn of Hope

Secondo

Kevin Olson

Calmly (♩= 132)

Play both hands one octave lower throughout

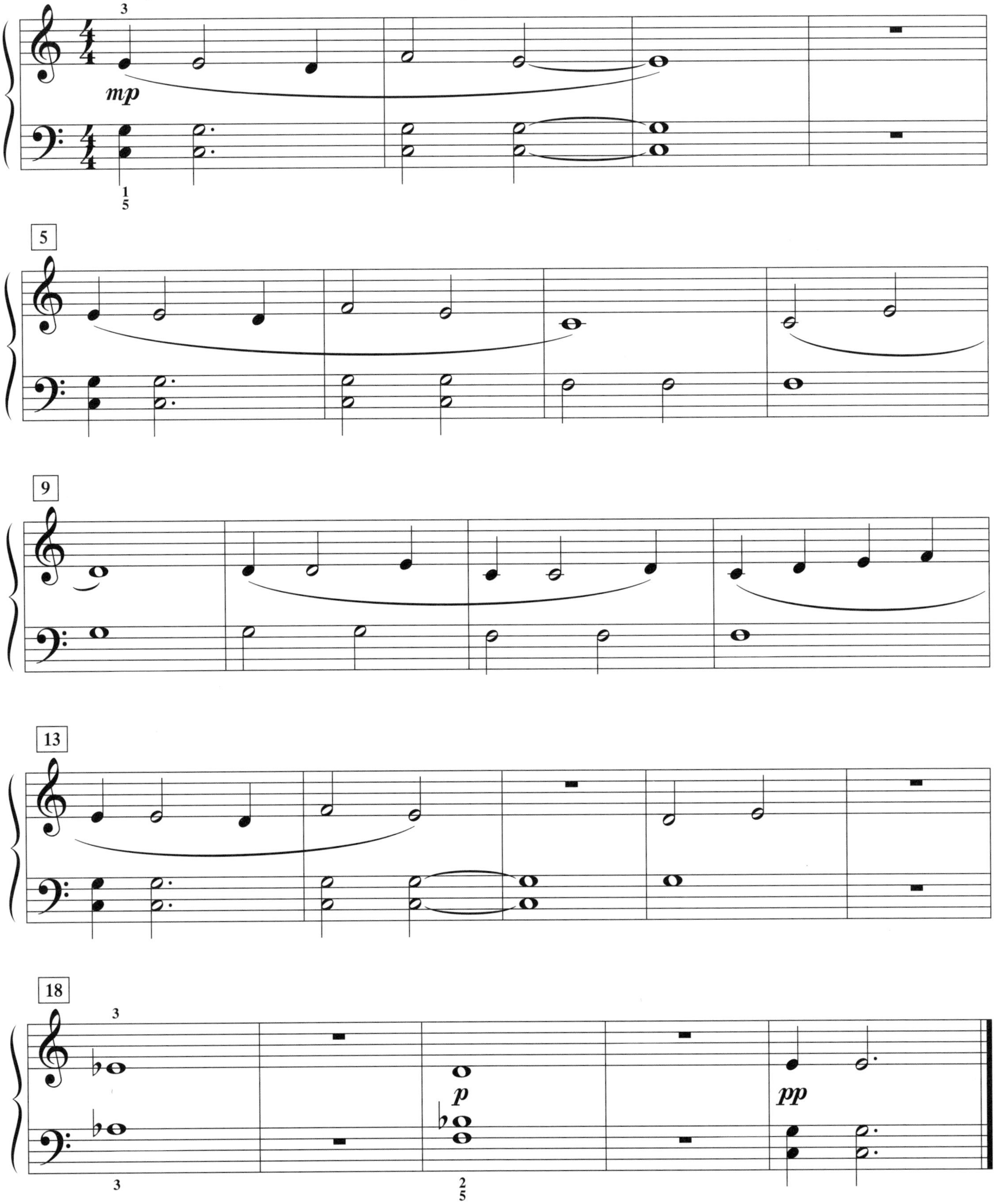

Hymn of Hope

Primo

Kevin Olson

Calmly (♩= 132) *Play both hands as written throughout*

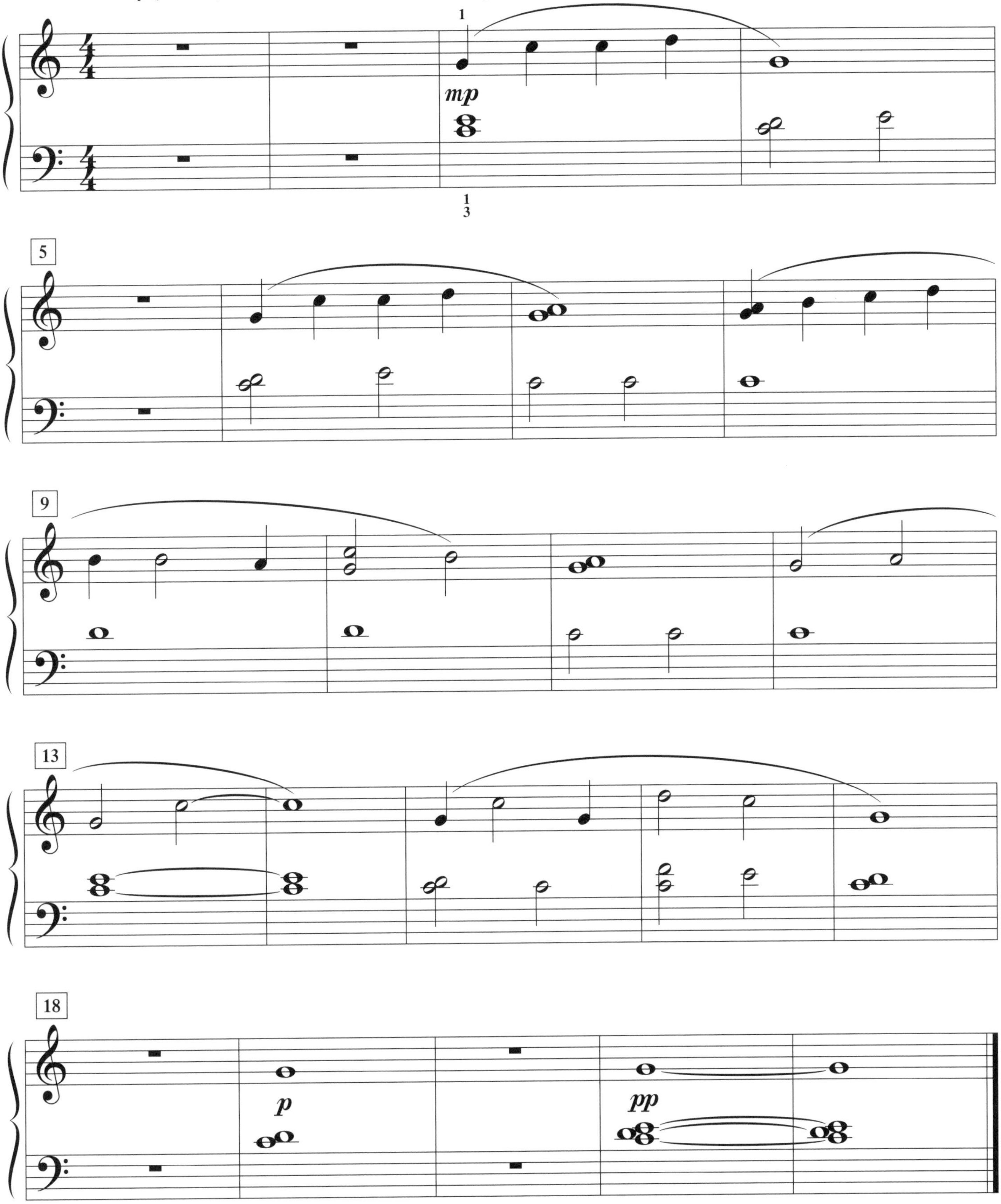

Wild Dance

Secondo

Edwin McLean

With a driving beat (𝅗𝅥 = ca. 104-116)

Play both hands one octave lower throughout

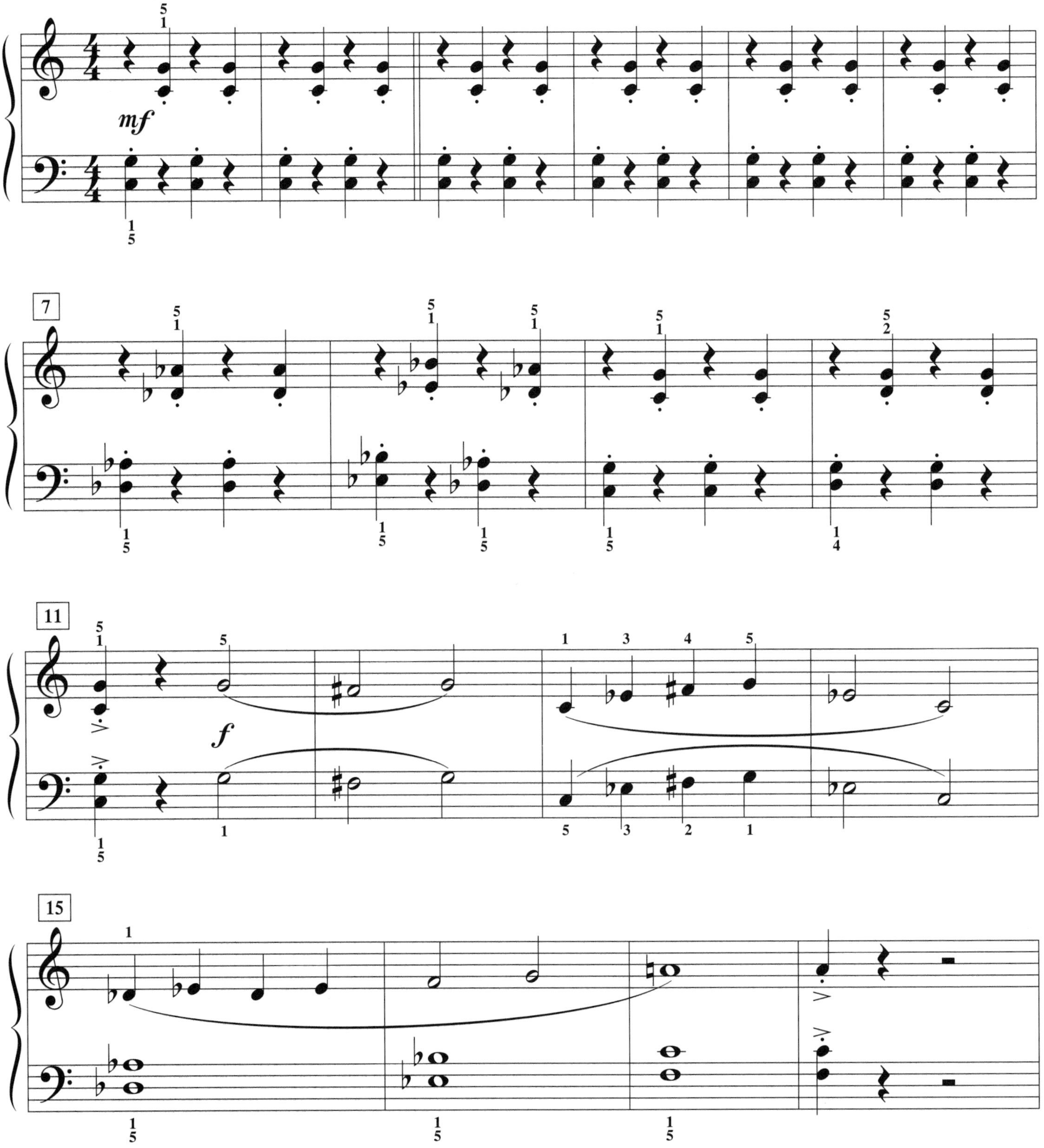

Wild Dance

Primo

Edwin McLean

With a driving beat (𝅗𝅥 = ca. 104-116)

Play both hands one octave higher

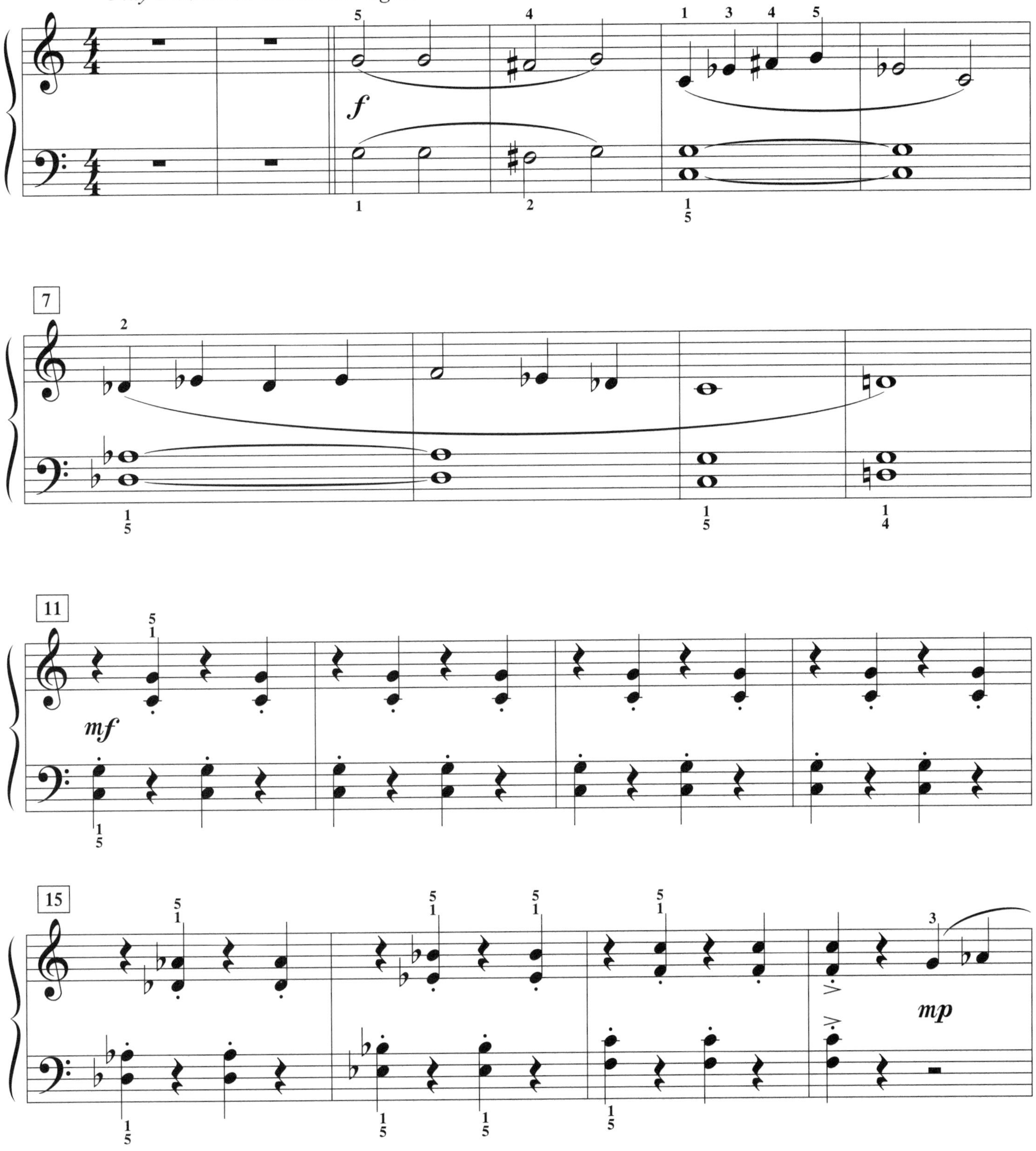

Secondo

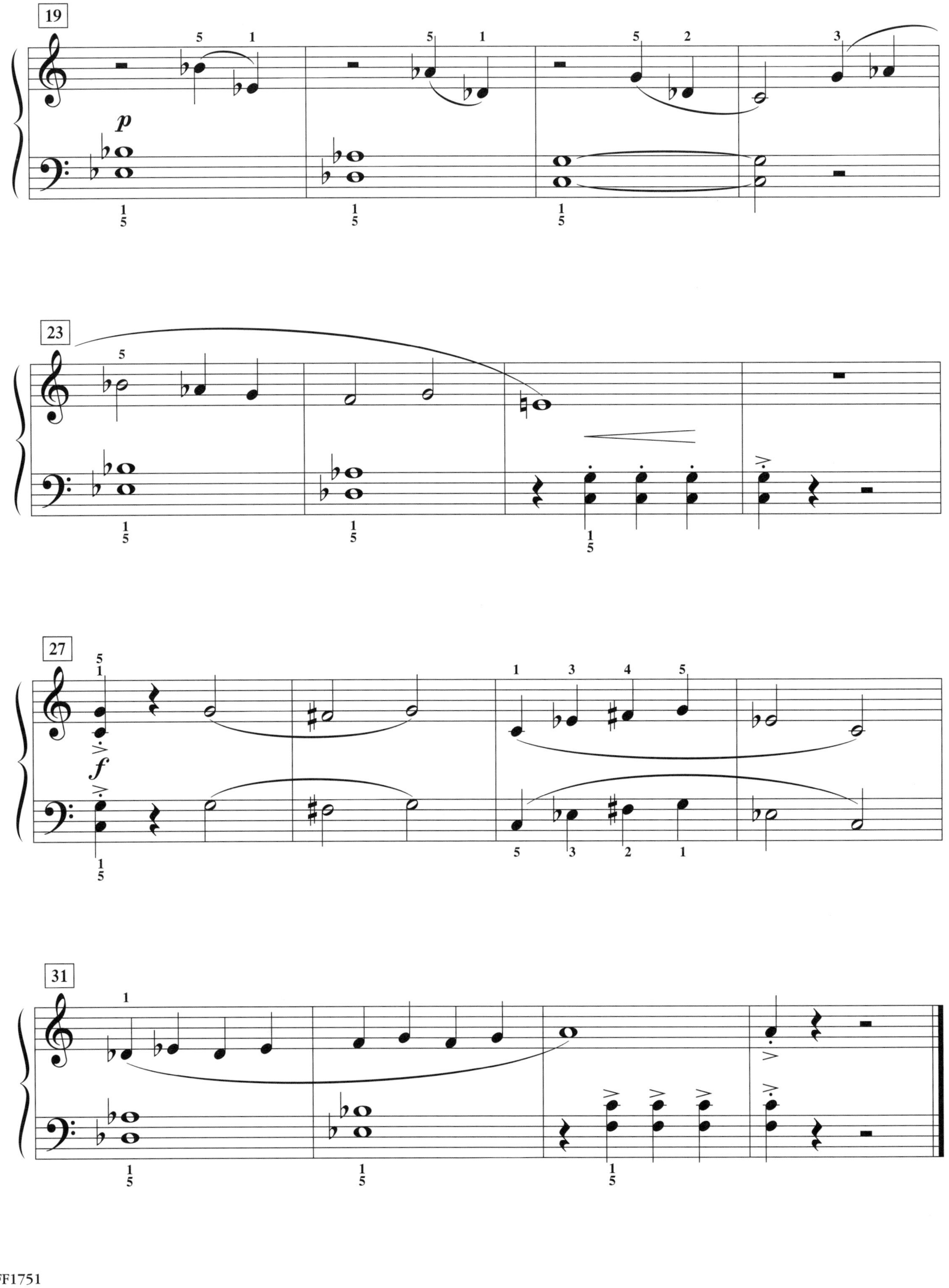

Primo

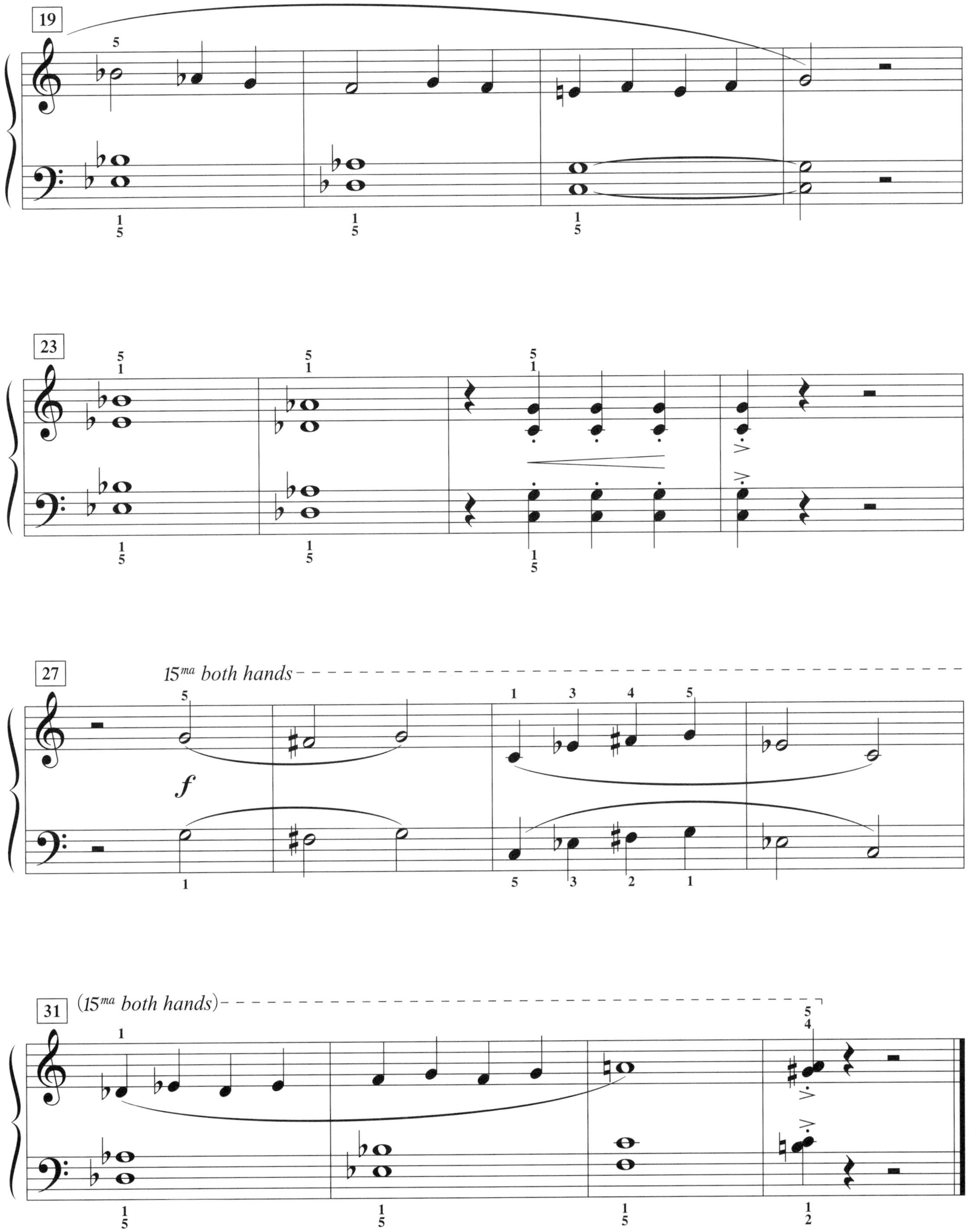

When the Saints Go Marching In

Secondo

Traditional Spiritual
arr. Edwin McLean

Lively march (𝅗𝅥 = ca. 104)
Play both hands one octave lower throughout

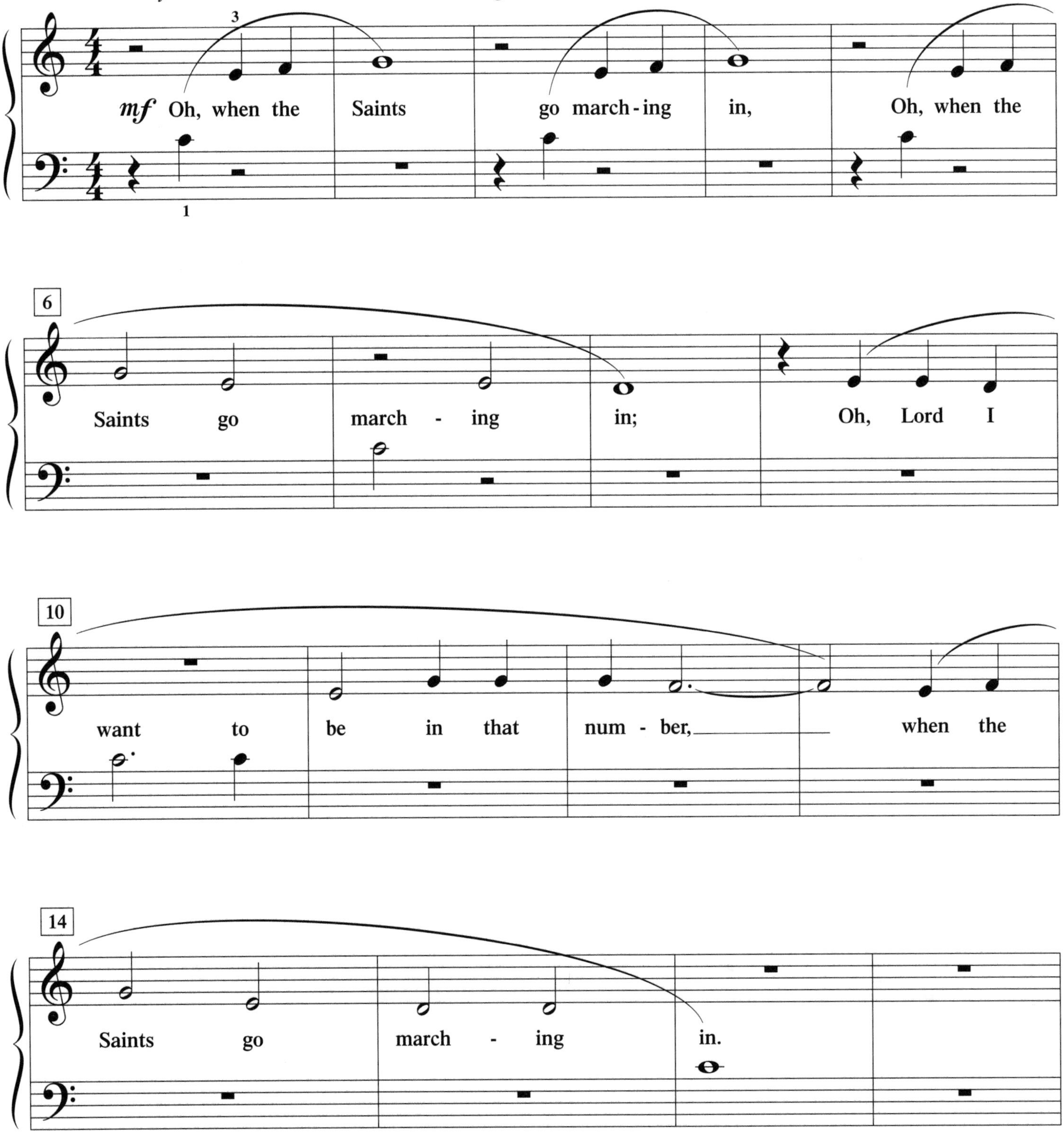

When the Saints Go Marching In

Primo

Traditional Spiritual
arr. Edwin McLean

Lively march (𝅗𝅥 = ca. 104)
Play both hands one octave higher throughout

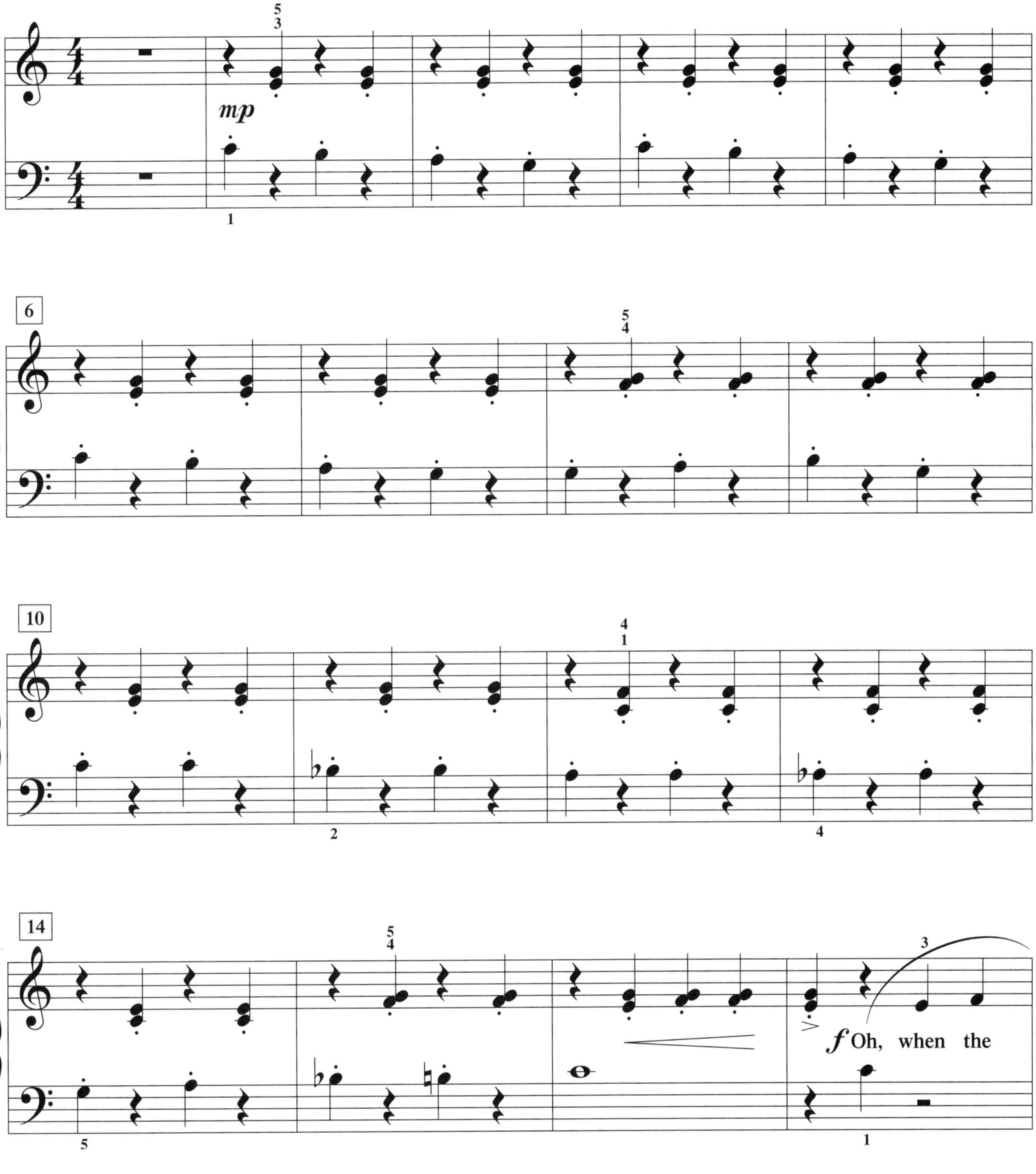

Secondo

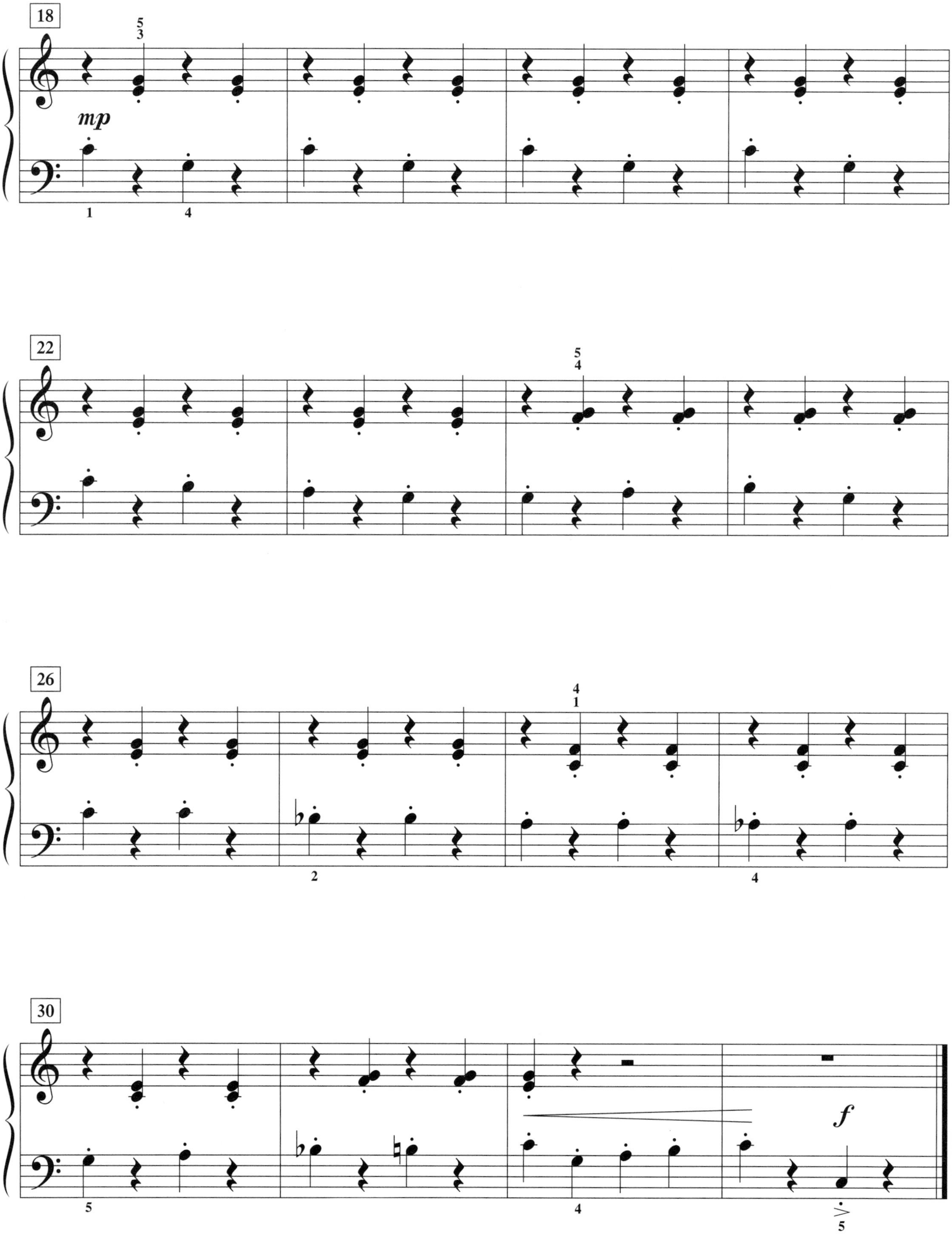

Primo

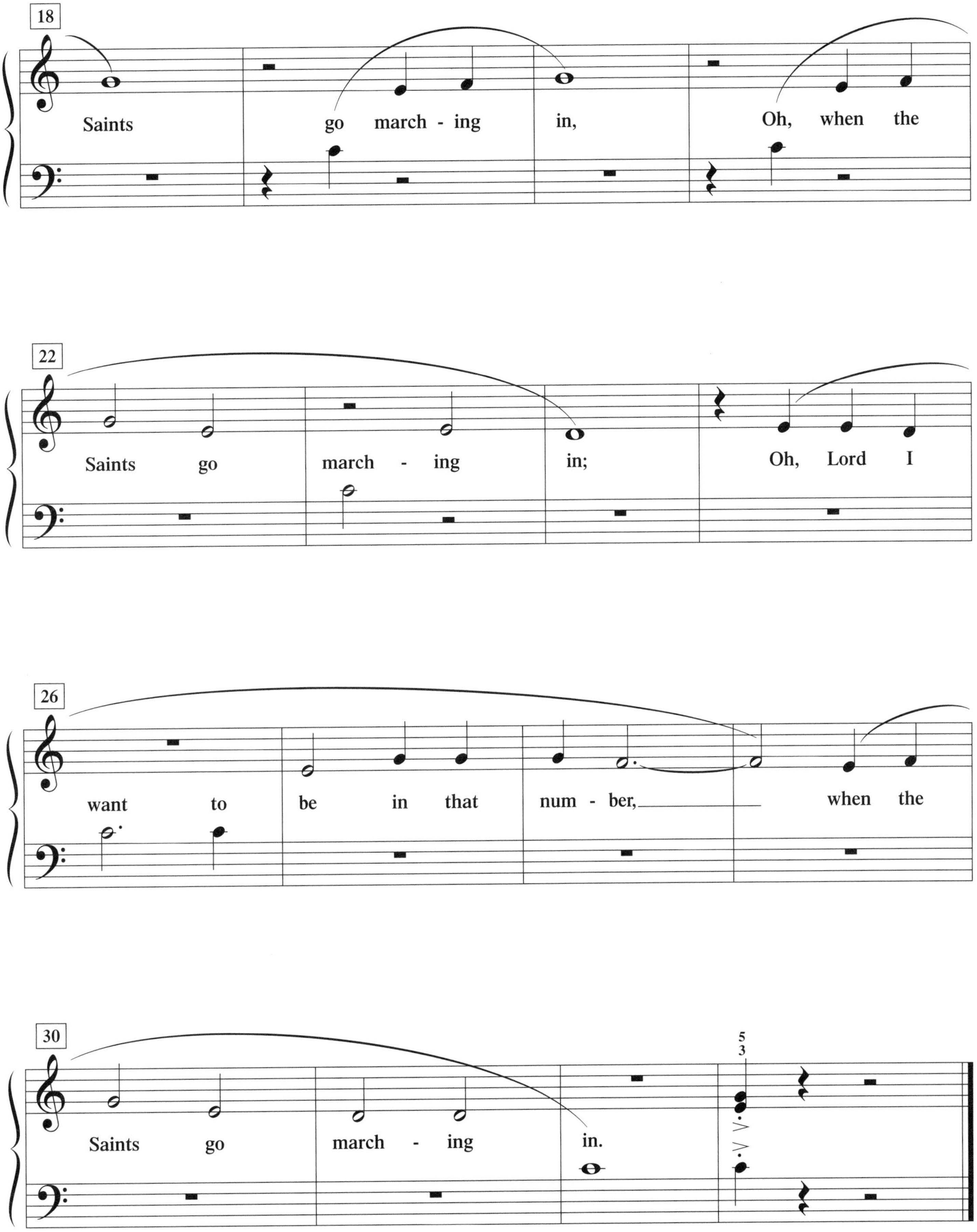
18
Saints go march - ing in, Oh, when the
22
Saints go march - ing in; Oh, Lord I
26
want to be in that num - ber, when the
30
Saints go march - ing in.
5
3

Aura Lee

Secondo

Words: George R. Poulton
Music: William Whiteman Fosdick
arr. Robert Schultz

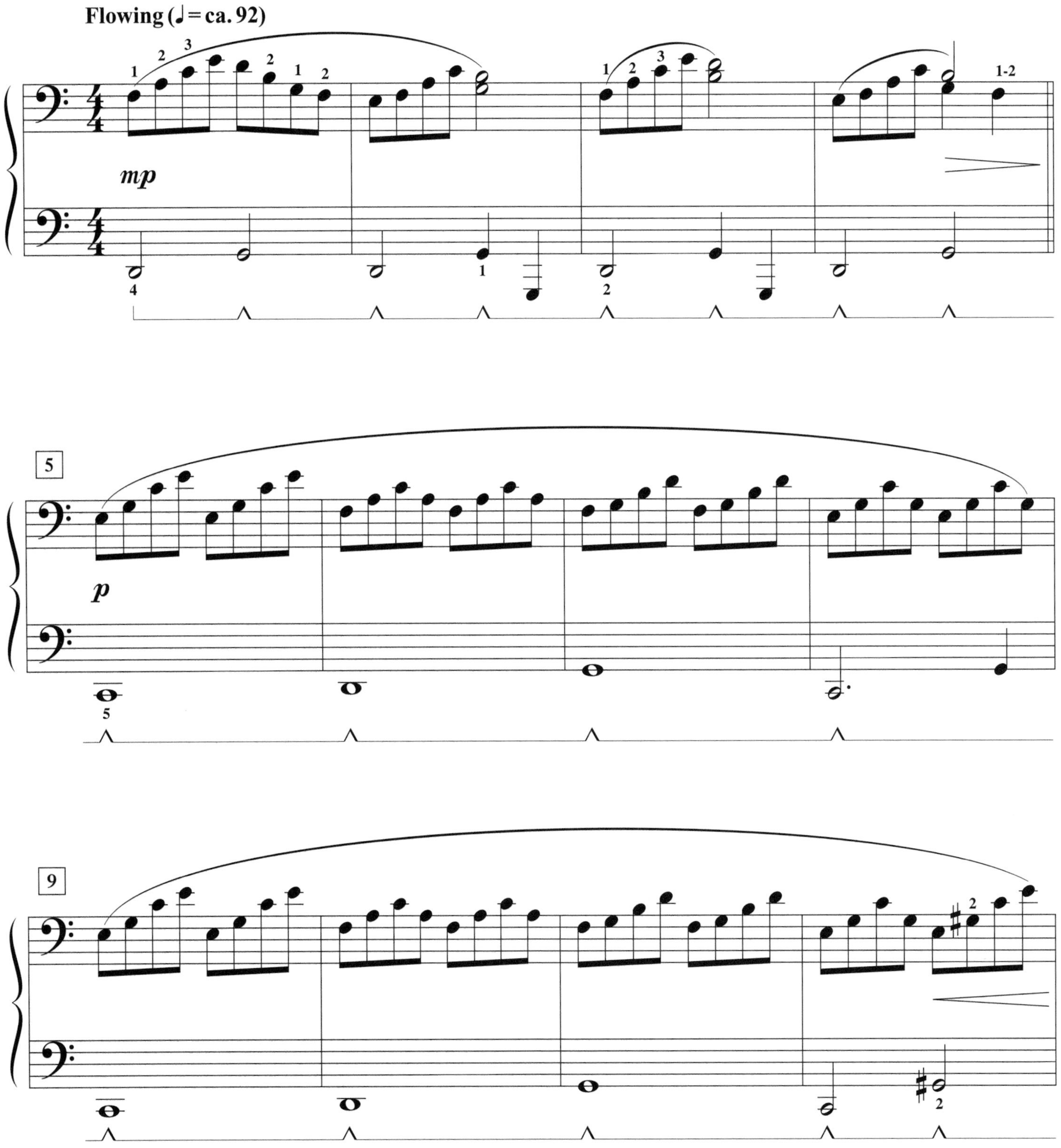

Aura Lee

Primo

Words: George R. Poulton
Music: William Whiteman Fosdick
arr. Robert Schultz

Flowing (♩ = ca. 92)
Play both hands one octave higher throughout

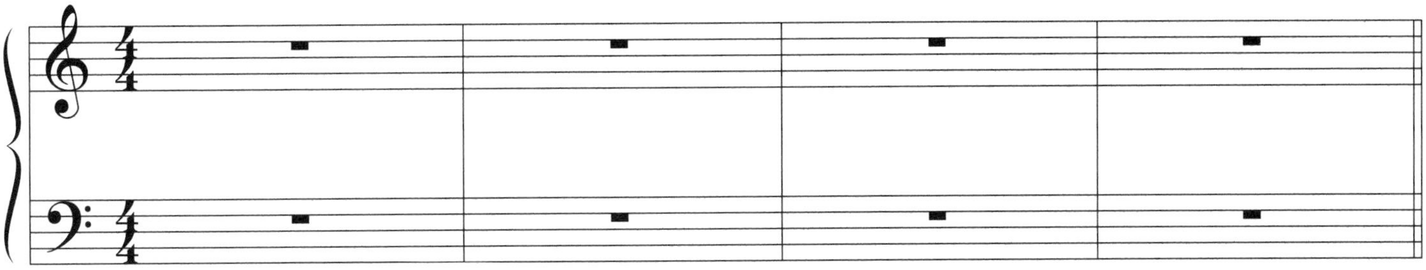

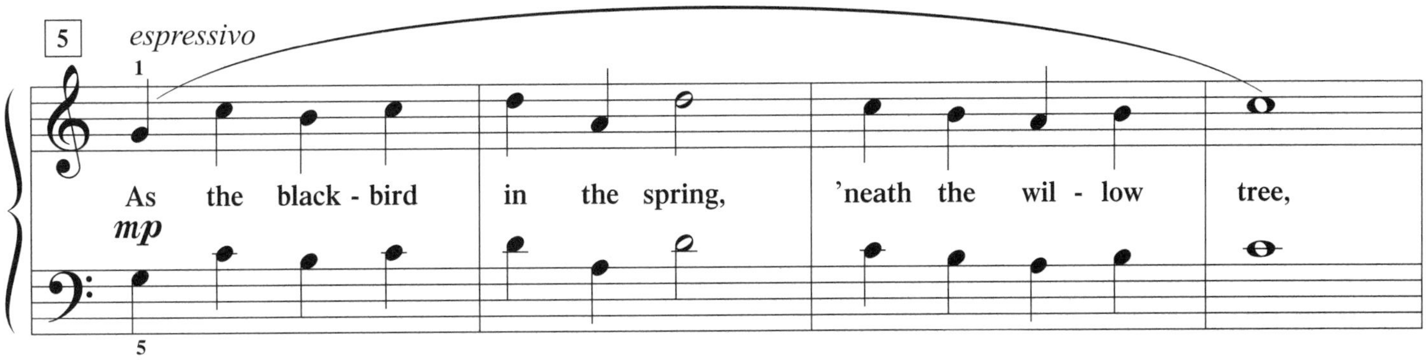
5
espressivo
As the black - bird in the spring, 'neath the wil - low tree,
mp

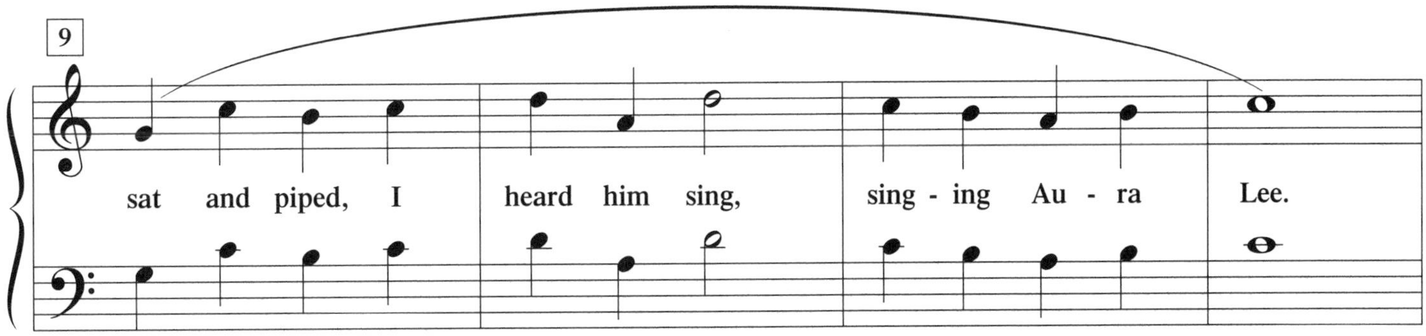
9
sat and piped, I heard him sing, sing - ing Au - ra Lee.

Secondo

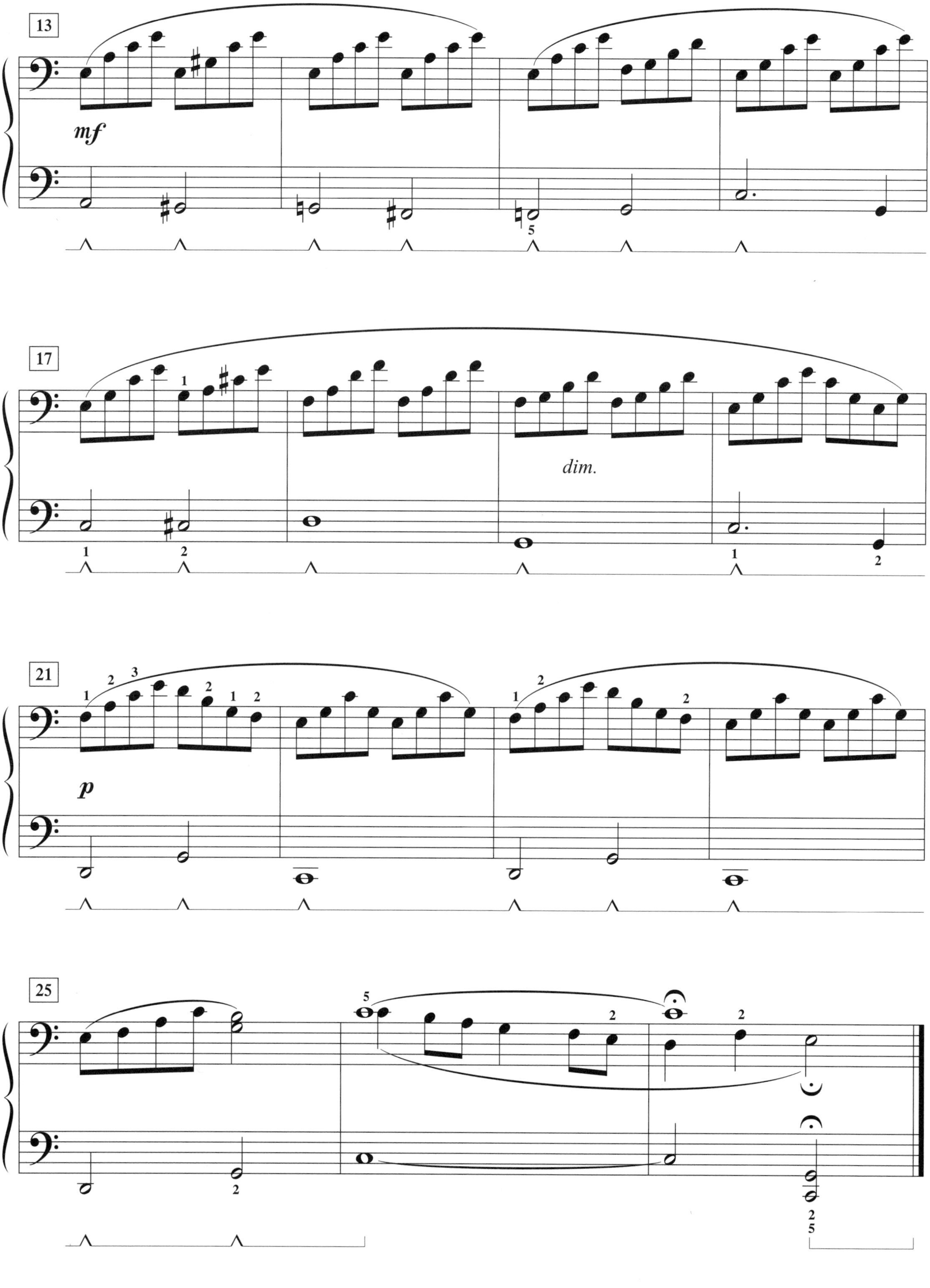

Primo

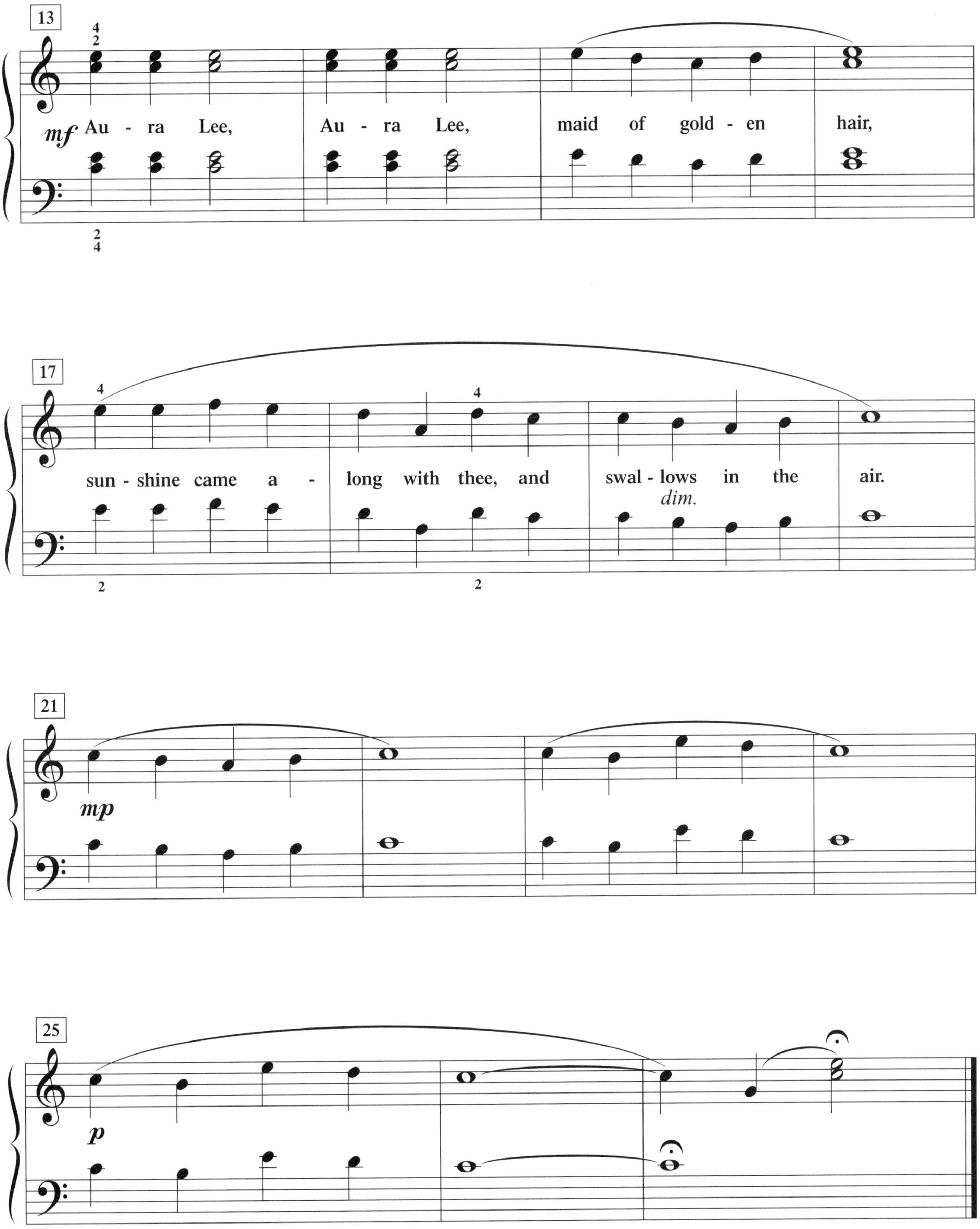
13
mf
Au - ra Lee, Au - ra Lee, maid of gold - en hair,
17
sun - shine came a - long with thee, and swal - lows in the air.
dim.
21
mp
25
p

The Dreamland Tree

(Lyrics inspired by the traditional nursery rhyme Sleep, Baby, Sleep)

Secondo

Timothy Brown

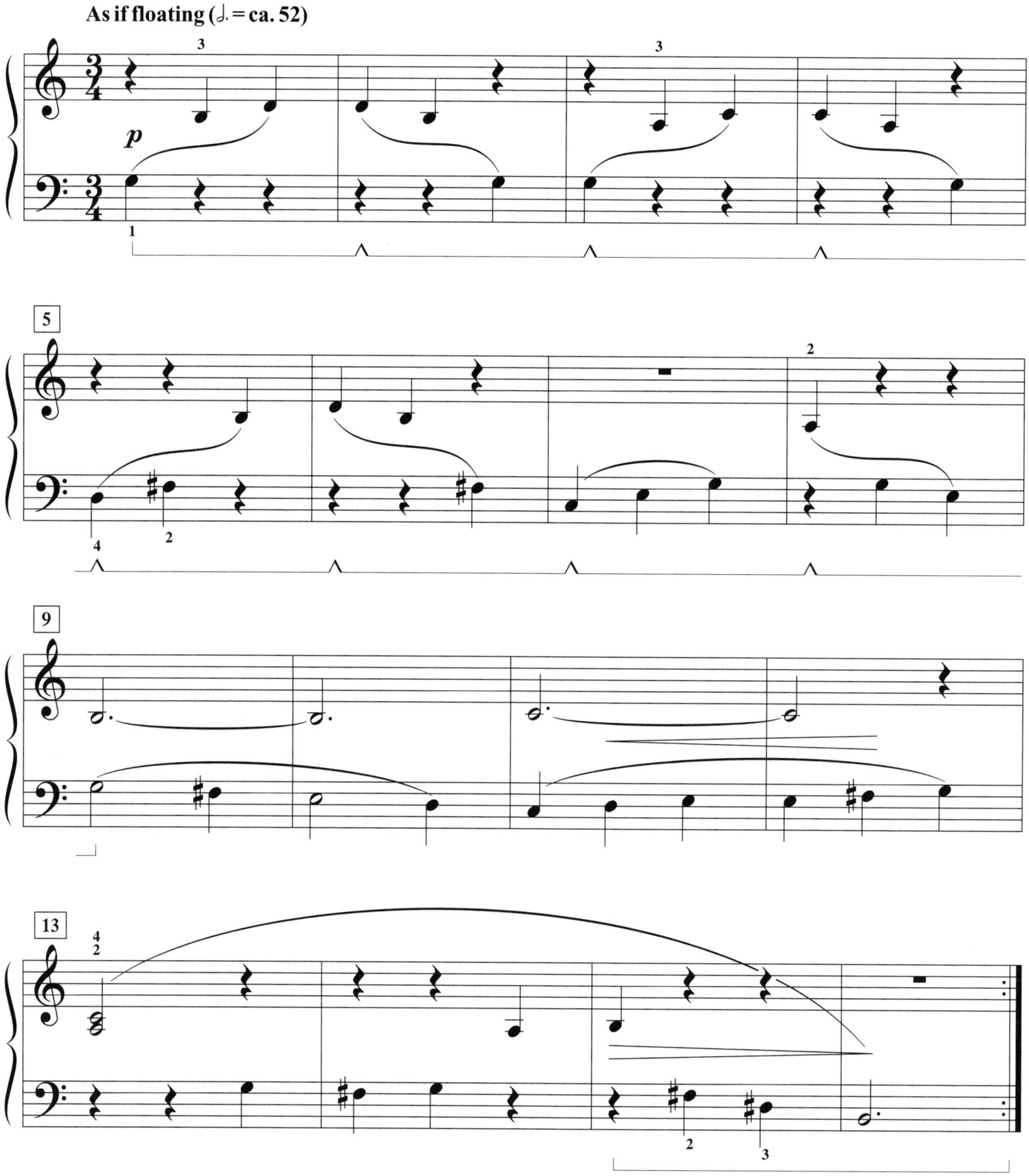

The Dreamland Tree

(Lyrics inspired by the traditional nursery rhyme Sleep, Baby, Sleep)

Primo

Timothy Brown

As if floating (𝅗𝅥. = ca. 52)
Play both hands one octave higher

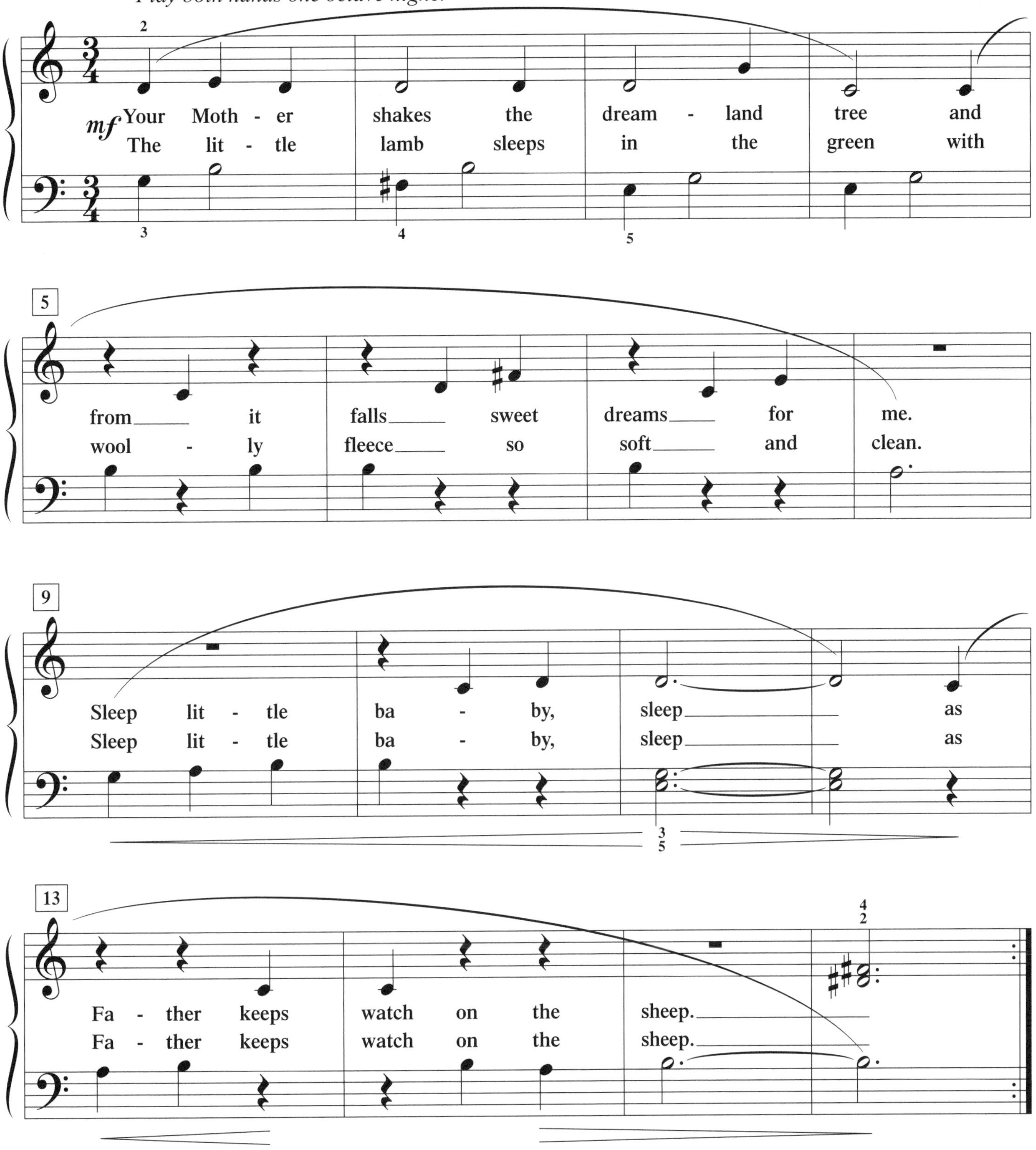

Secondo

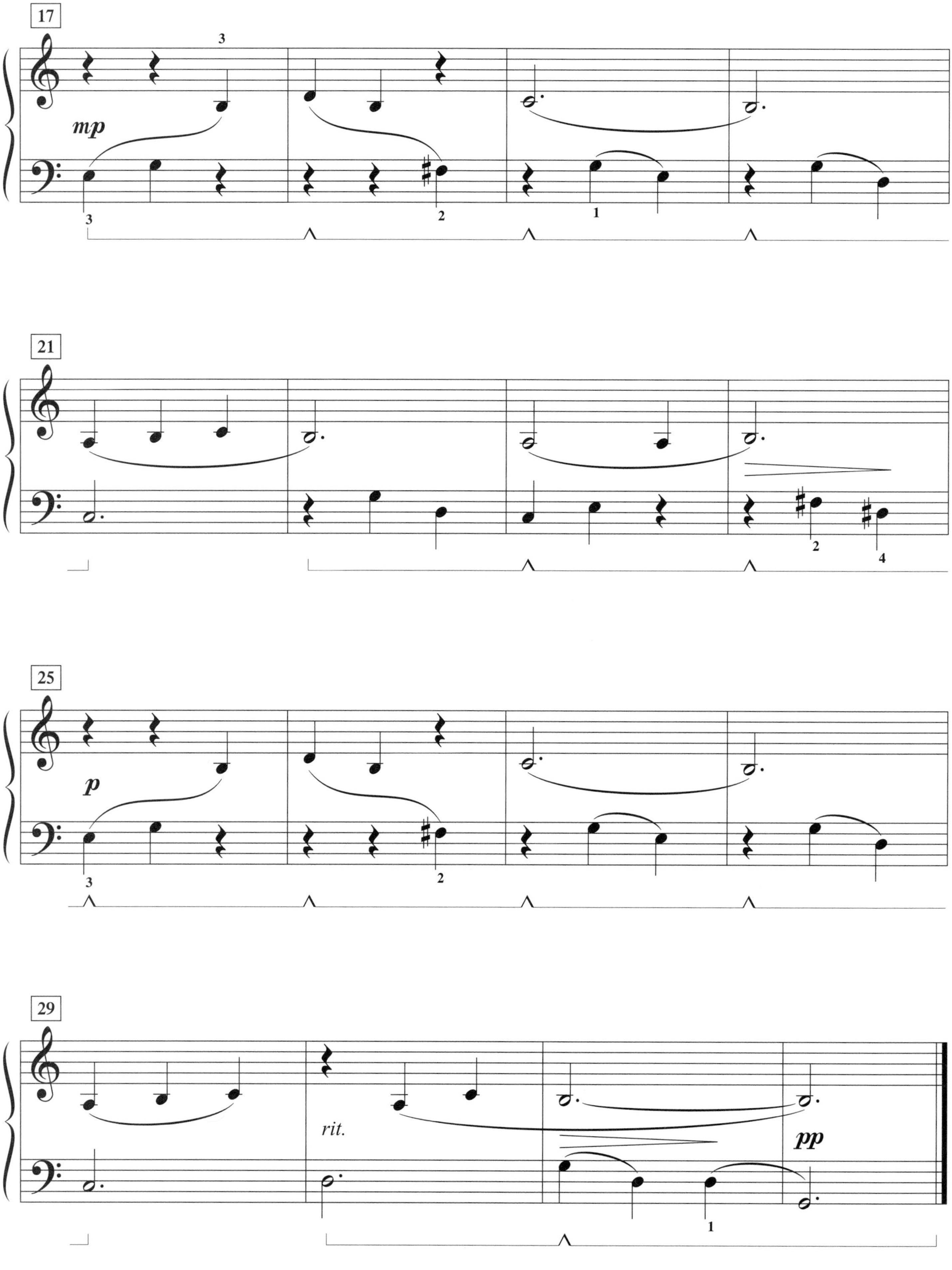

Primo

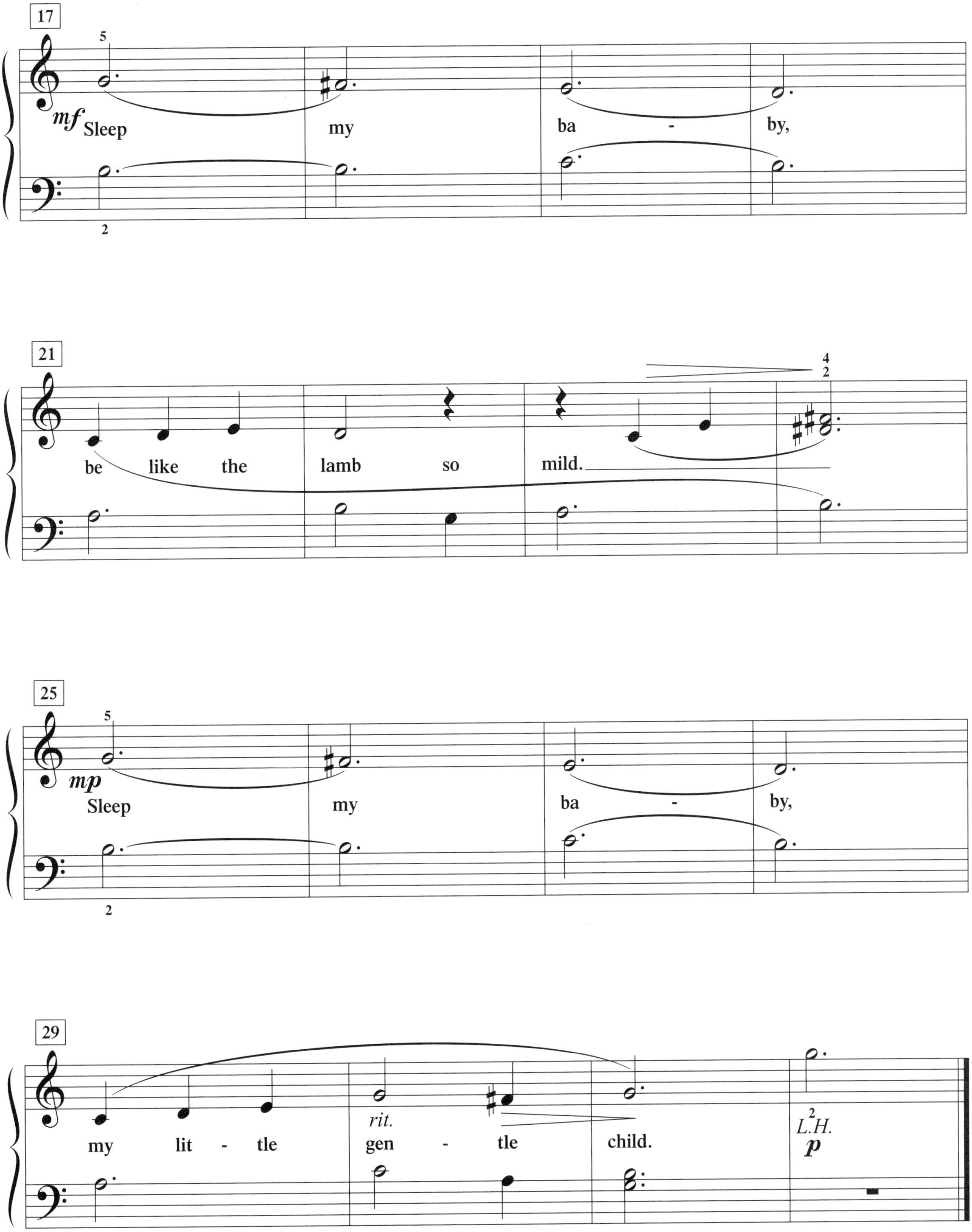
17
mf
Sleep my ba - by,
21
be like the lamb so mild.
25
mp
Sleep my ba - by,
29
my lit - tle gen - tle child.
rit.
L.H.
p

Simple Gifts

Secondo

Shaker Elder Joseph Brackett, Jr.
arr. Kevin Olson

Gently flowing (♩= ca. 120)

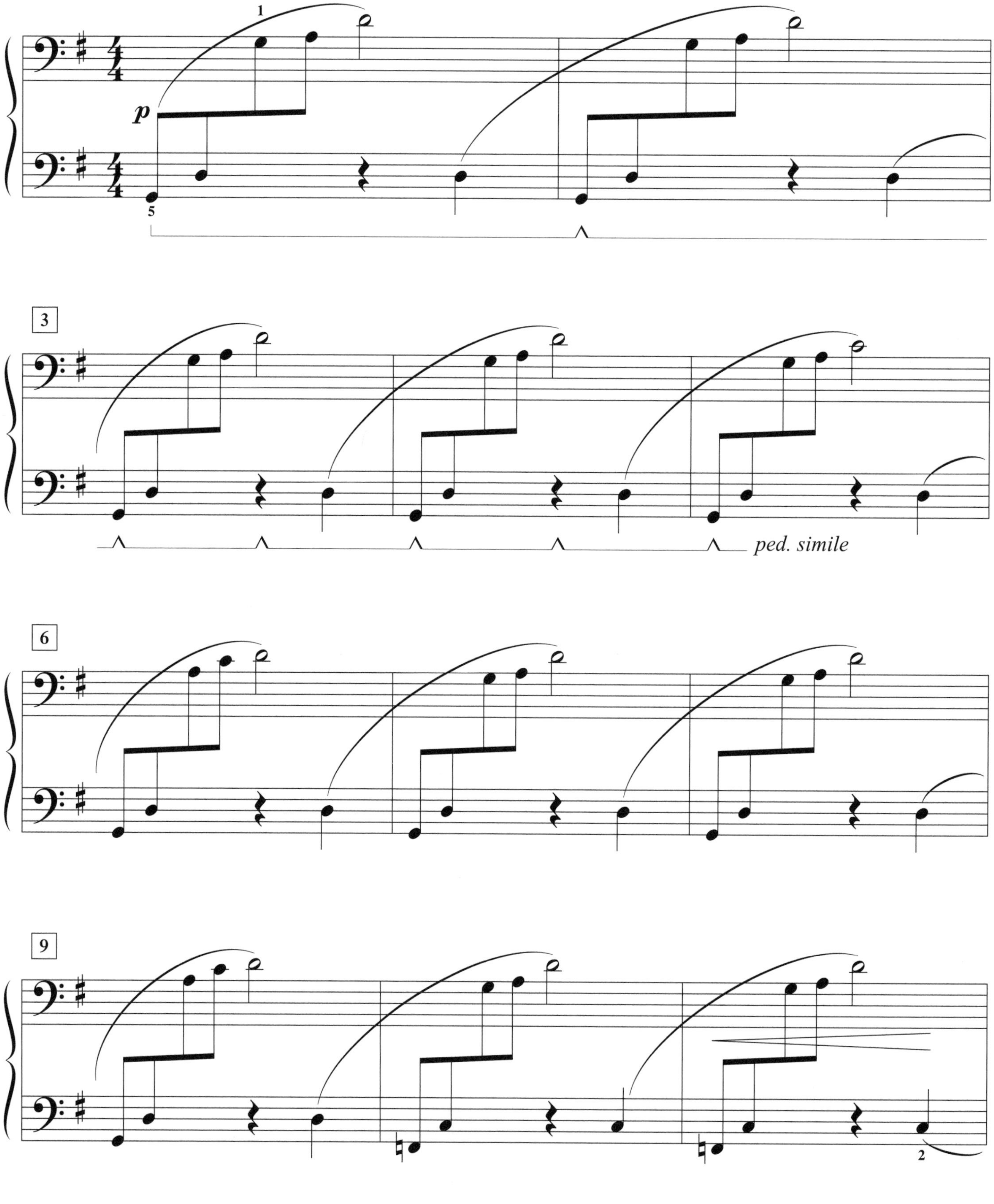

Simple Gifts

Primo

Shaker Elder Joseph Brackett, Jr.
arr. Kevin Olson

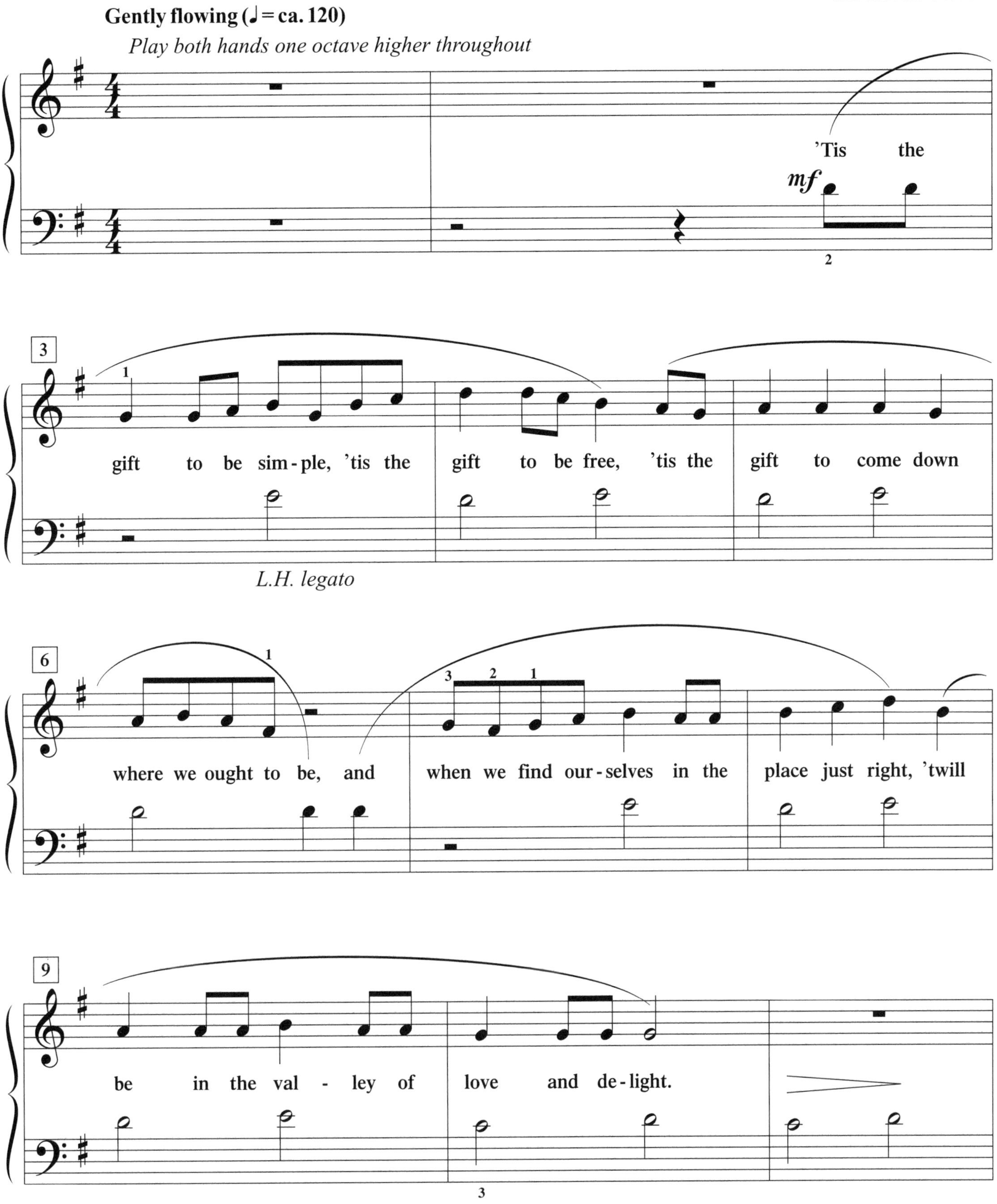
Gently flowing (♩= ca. 120)
Play both hands one octave higher throughout
'Tis the
mf
3
gift to be sim-ple, 'tis the gift to be free, 'tis the gift to come down
L.H. legato
6
where we ought to be, and when we find our-selves in the place just right, 'twill
9
be in the val - ley of love and de-light.

Secondo

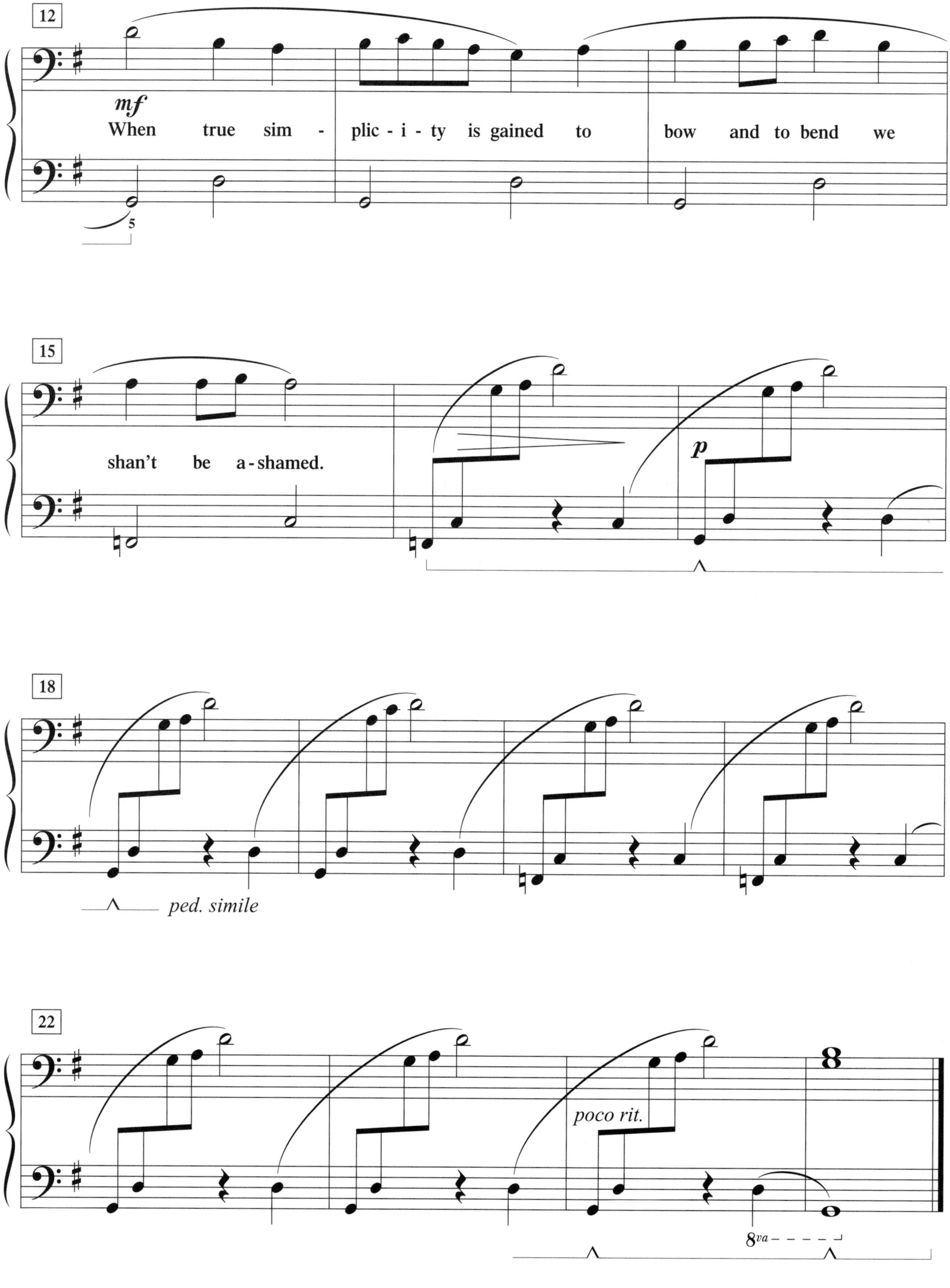
12
mf
When true sim - plic - i - ty is gained to bow and to bend we
5
15
shan't be a - shamed.
p
18
ped. simile
22
poco rit.
8va

Primo

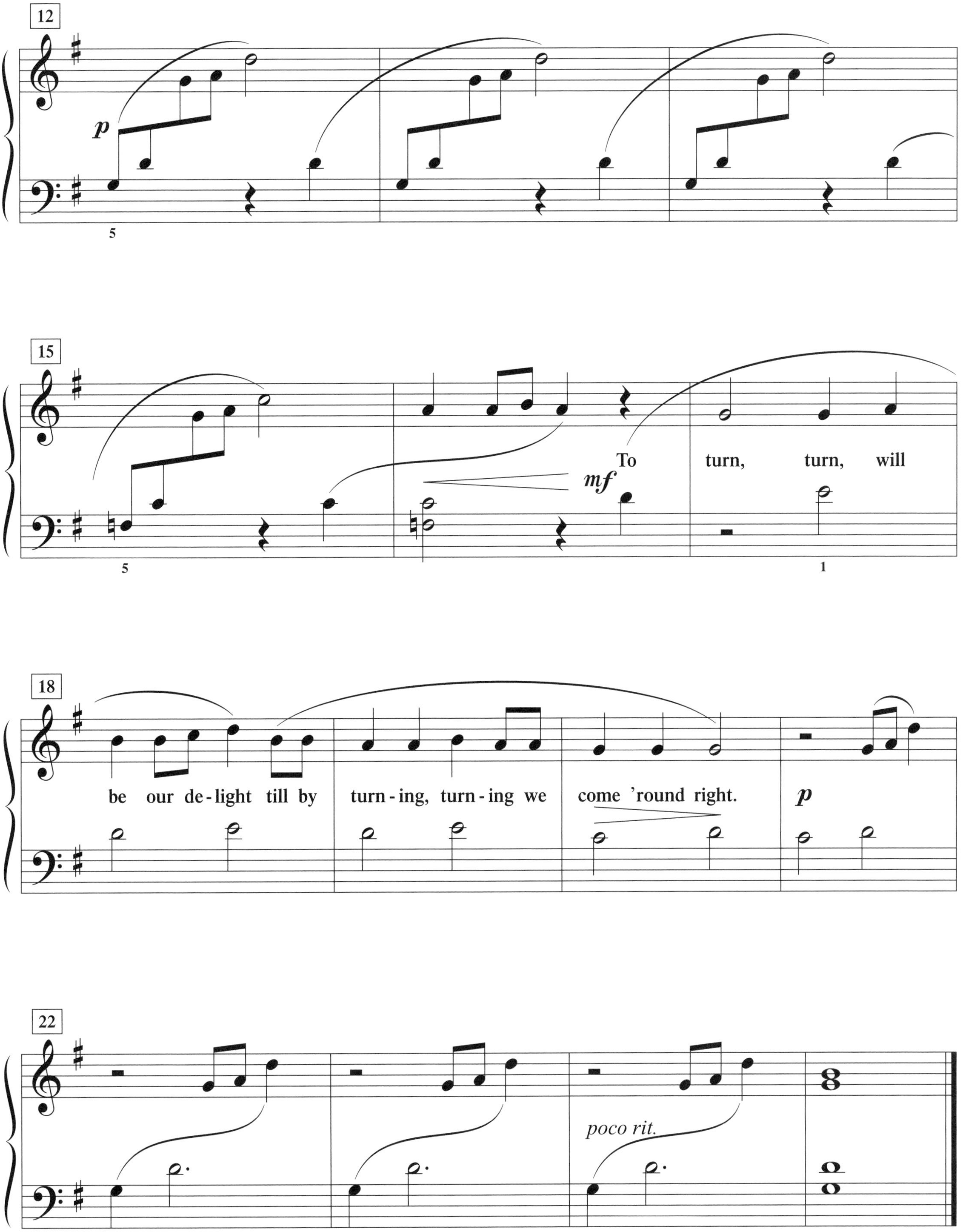
12
p
15
mf
To turn, turn, will
18
be our de-light till by
turn-ing, turn-ing we
come 'round right.
p
22
poco rit.

When Irish Eyes are Smiling

Secondo

Words: Chauncey Olcott & George Graff, Jr.
Music: Ernest R. Ball
arr. Melody Bober

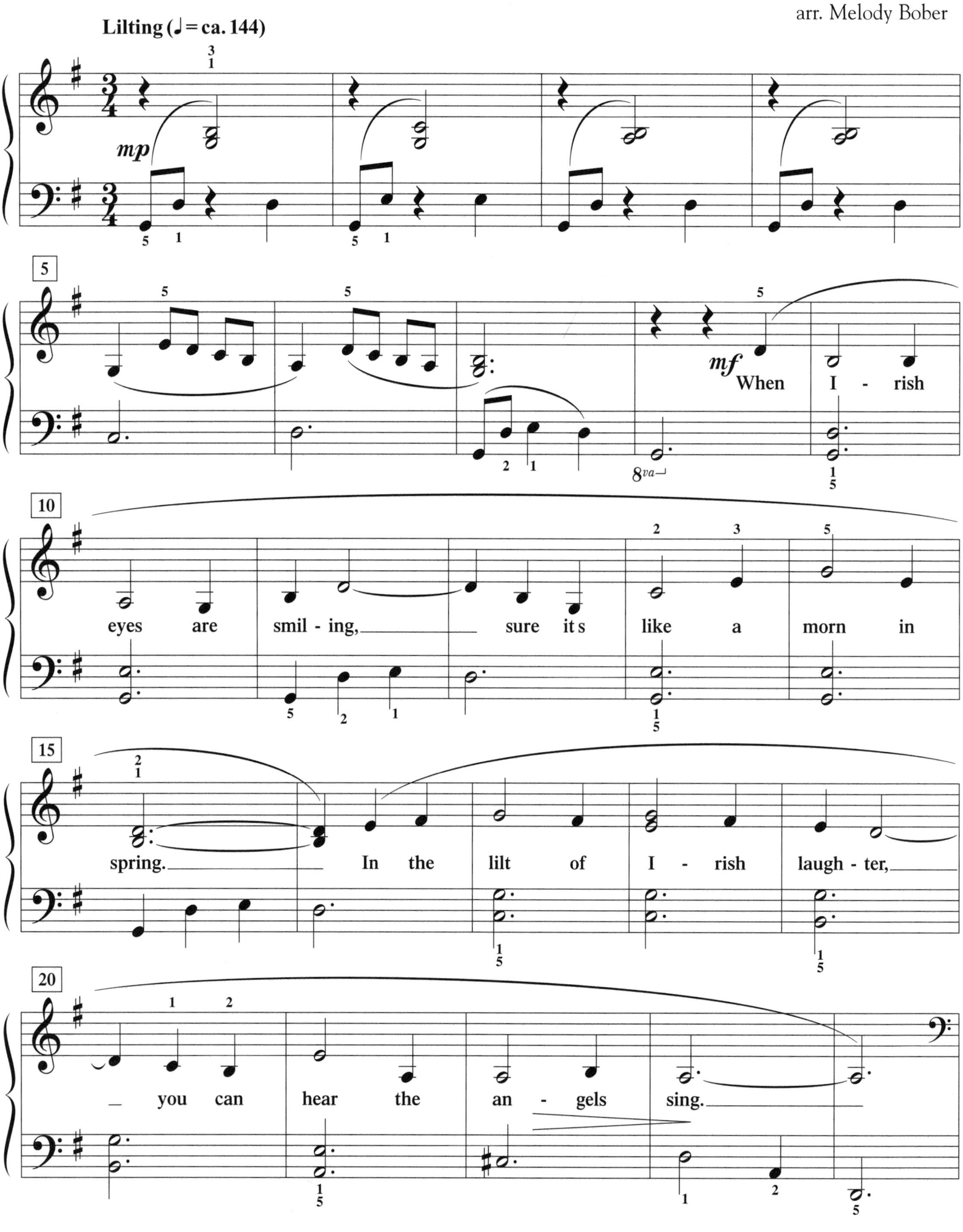

When Irish Eyes are Smiling

Primo

Words: Chauncey Olcott & George Graff, Jr.
Music: Ernest R. Ball
arr. Melody Bober

Lilting (♩= ca. 144)
Play both hands one octave higher throughout

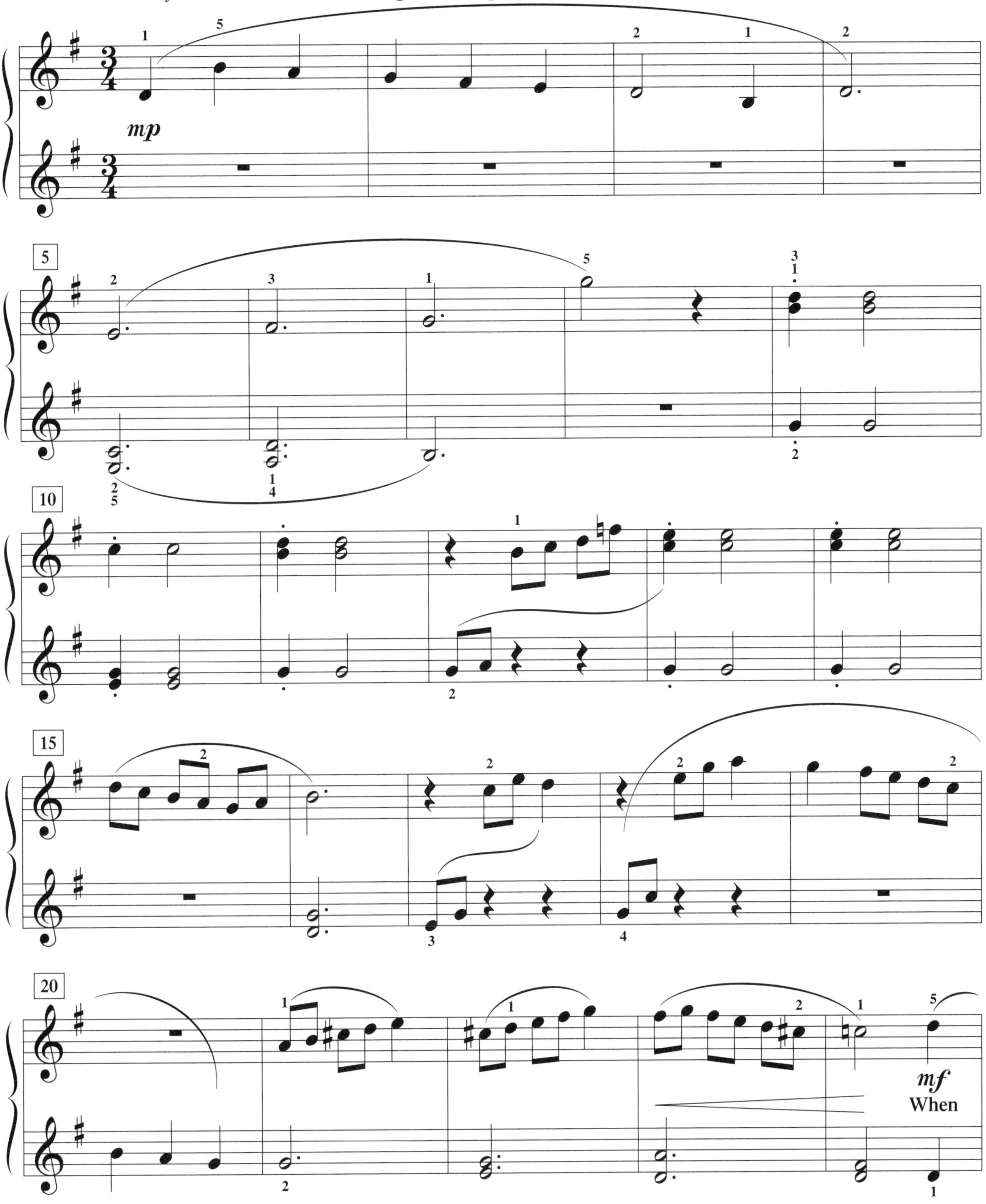

Secondo

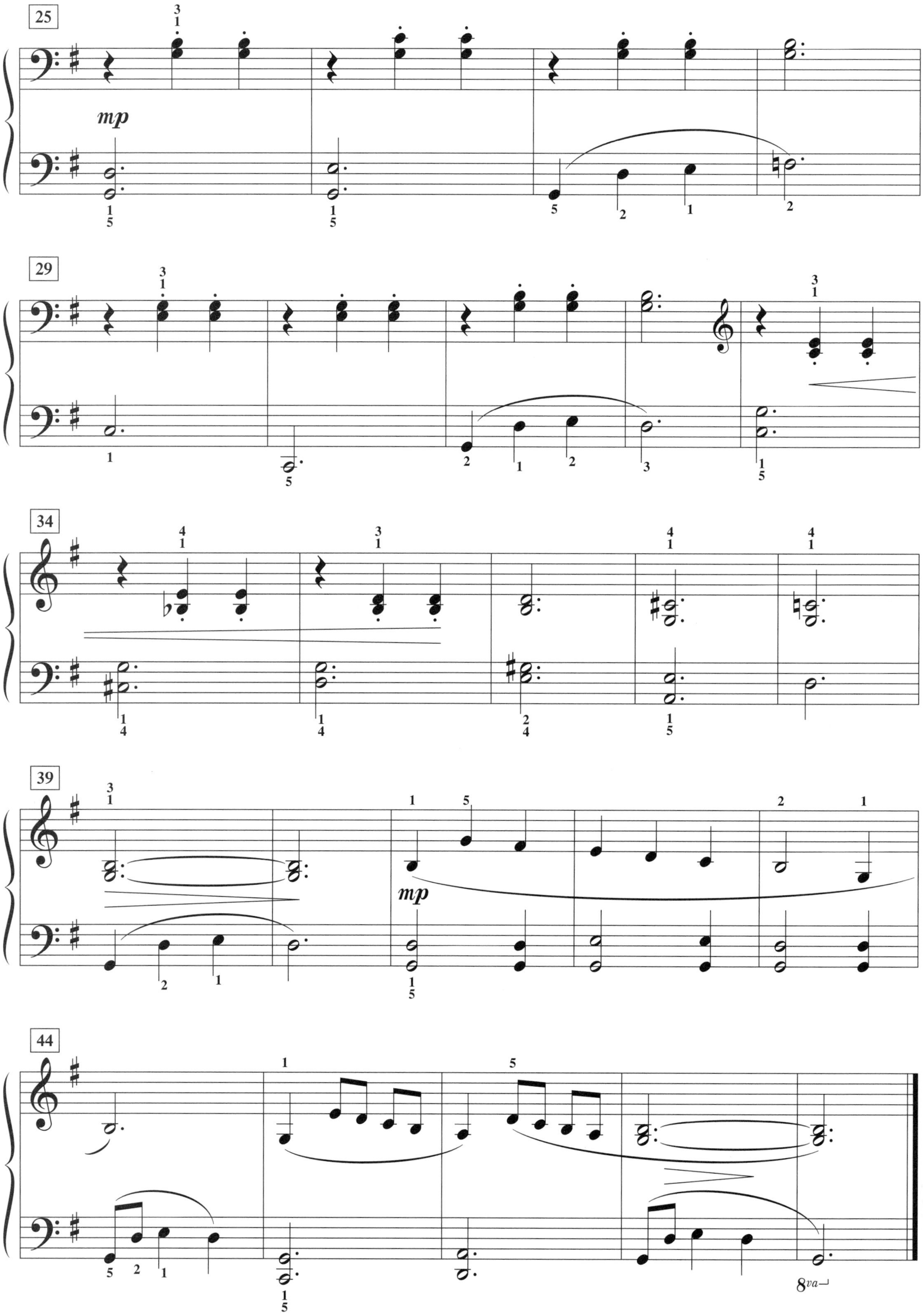

Primo

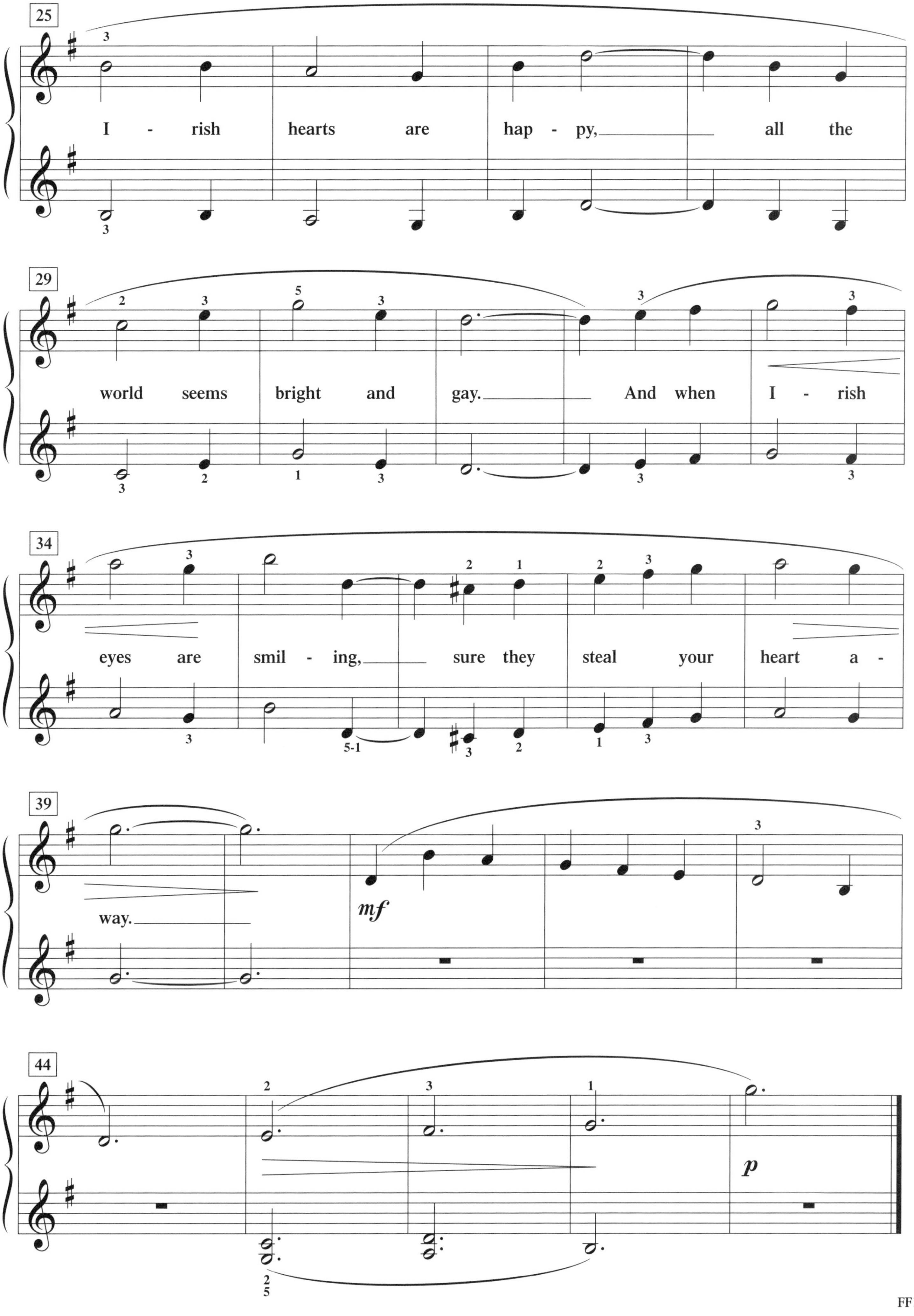
25
I - rish hearts are hap - py, all the
29
world seems bright and gay. And when I - rish
34
eyes are smil - ing, sure they steal your heart a -
39
way.
mf
44
p

Song of the Sahara

Secondo

Kevin Olson

Mysteriously (♩= 120-132)

Play both hands one octave lower throughout

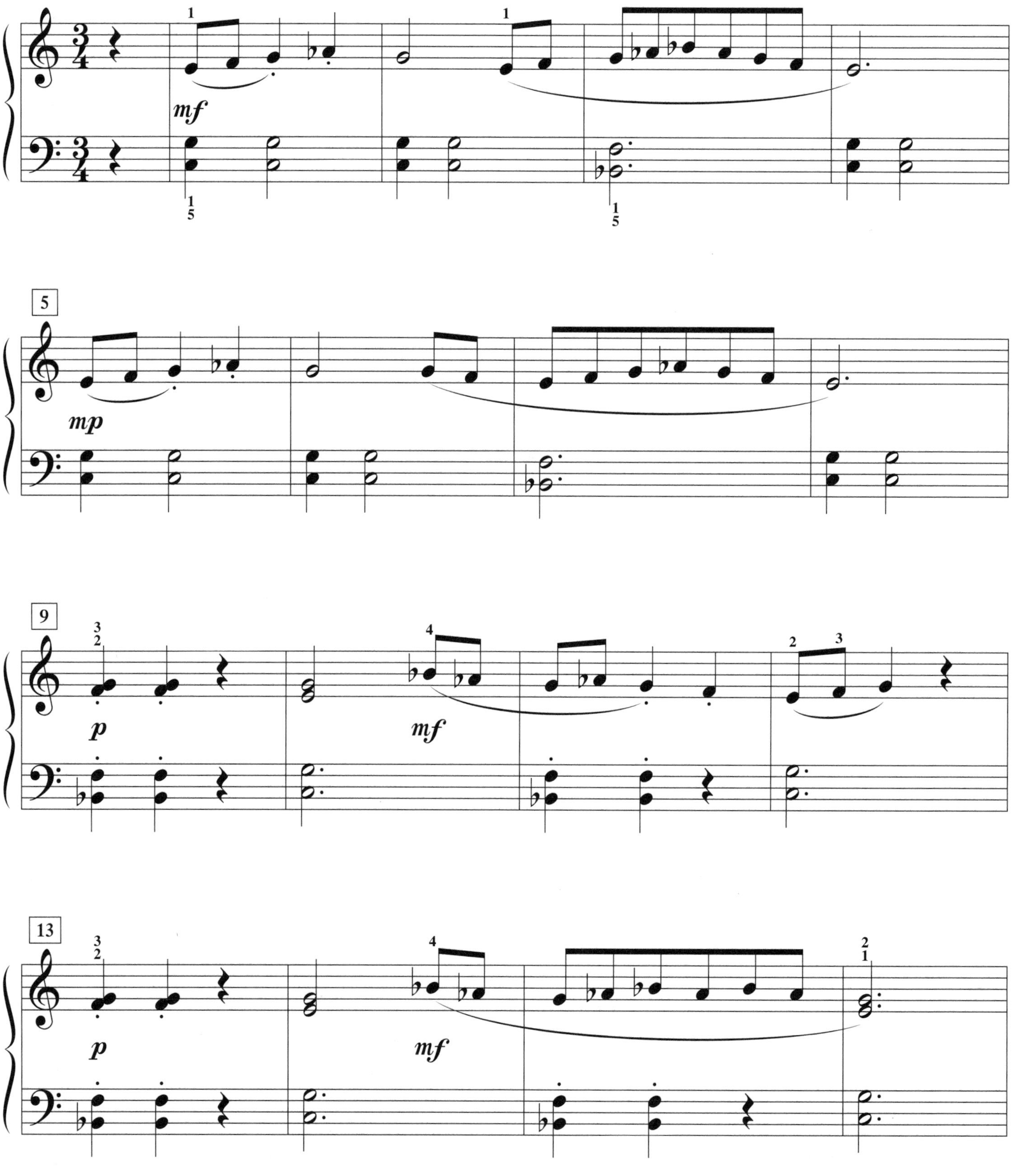

Song of the Sahara

Primo

Kevin Olson

Mysteriously (♩= 120-132)

Play both hands one octave higher throughout

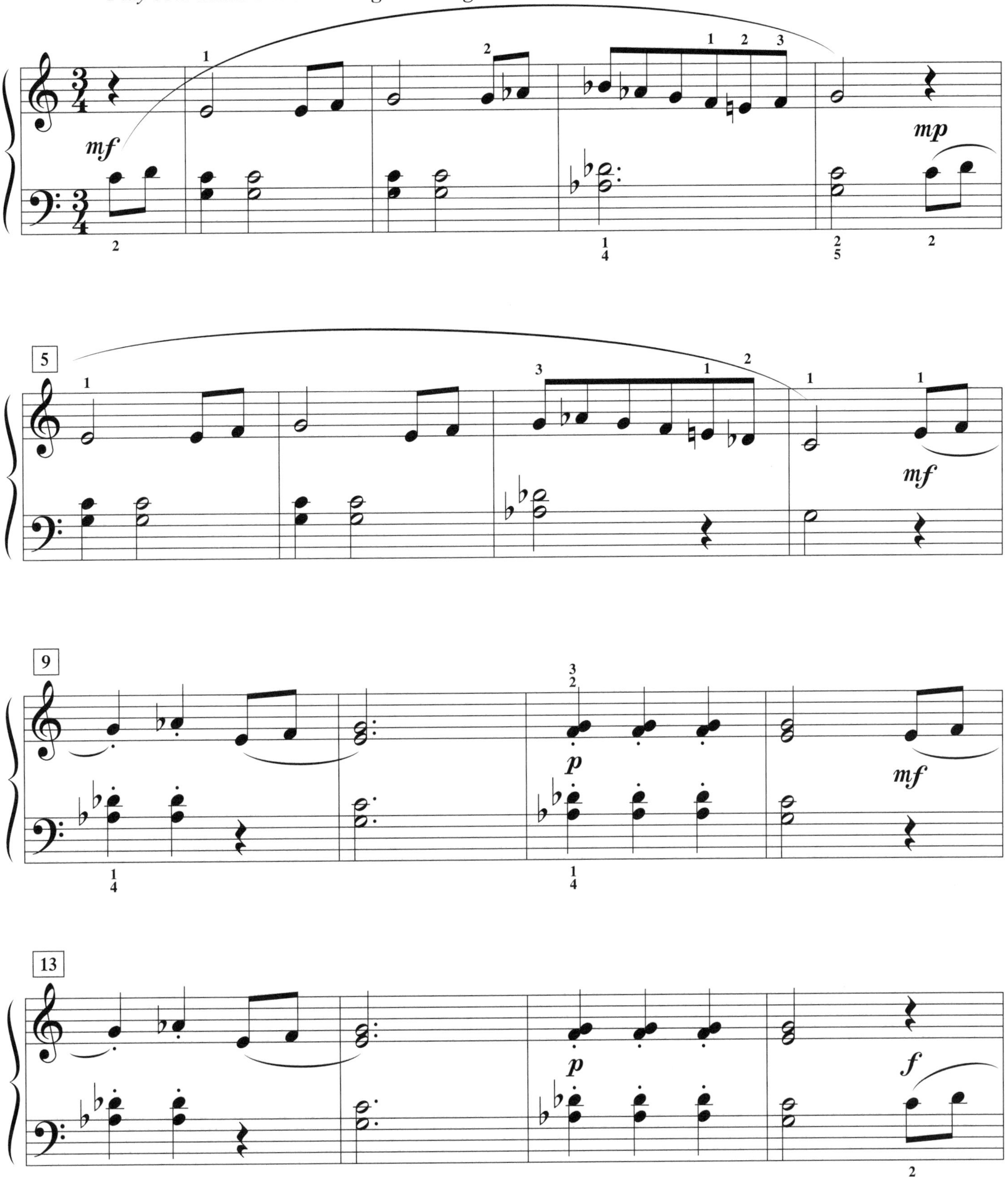

Secondo

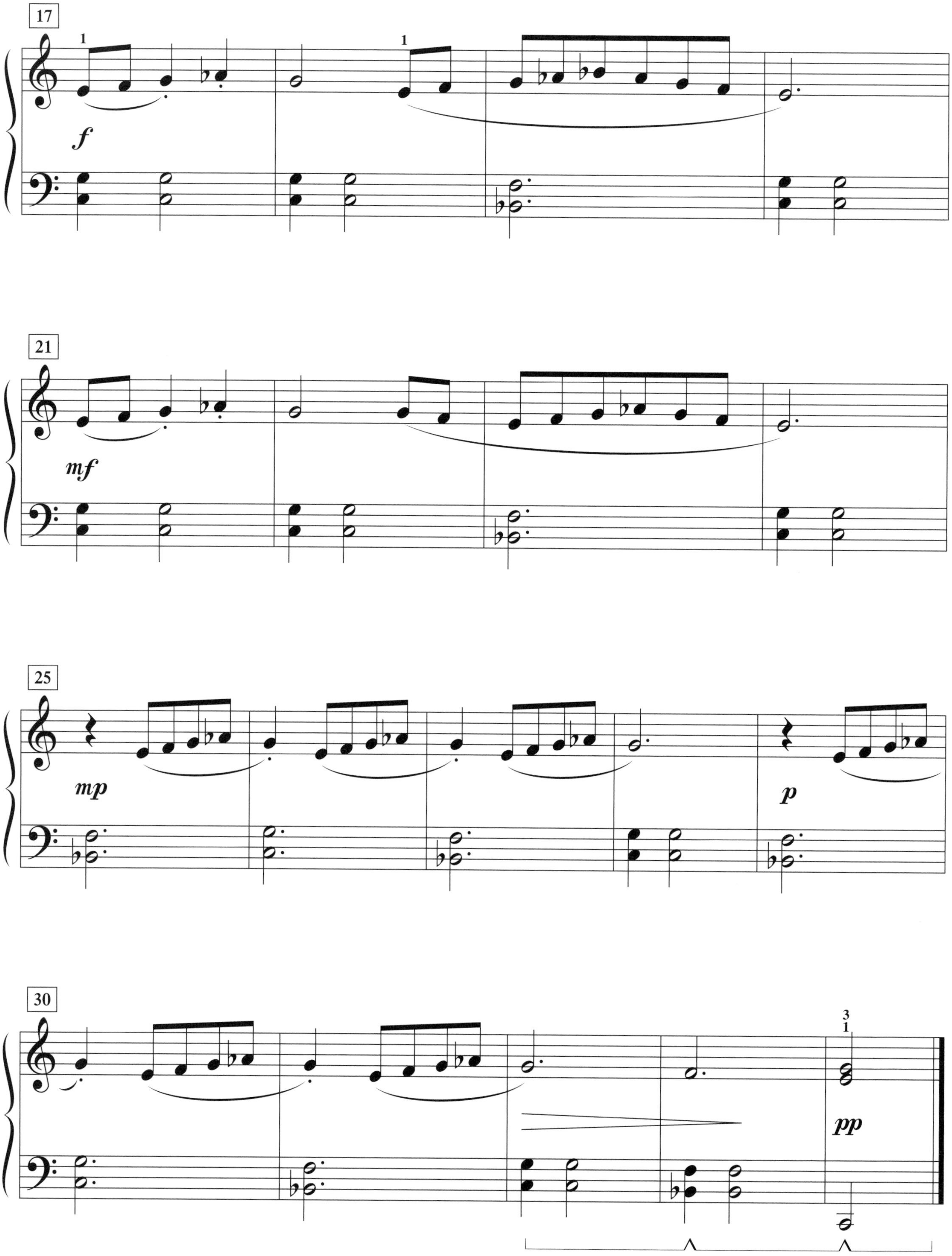

Primo

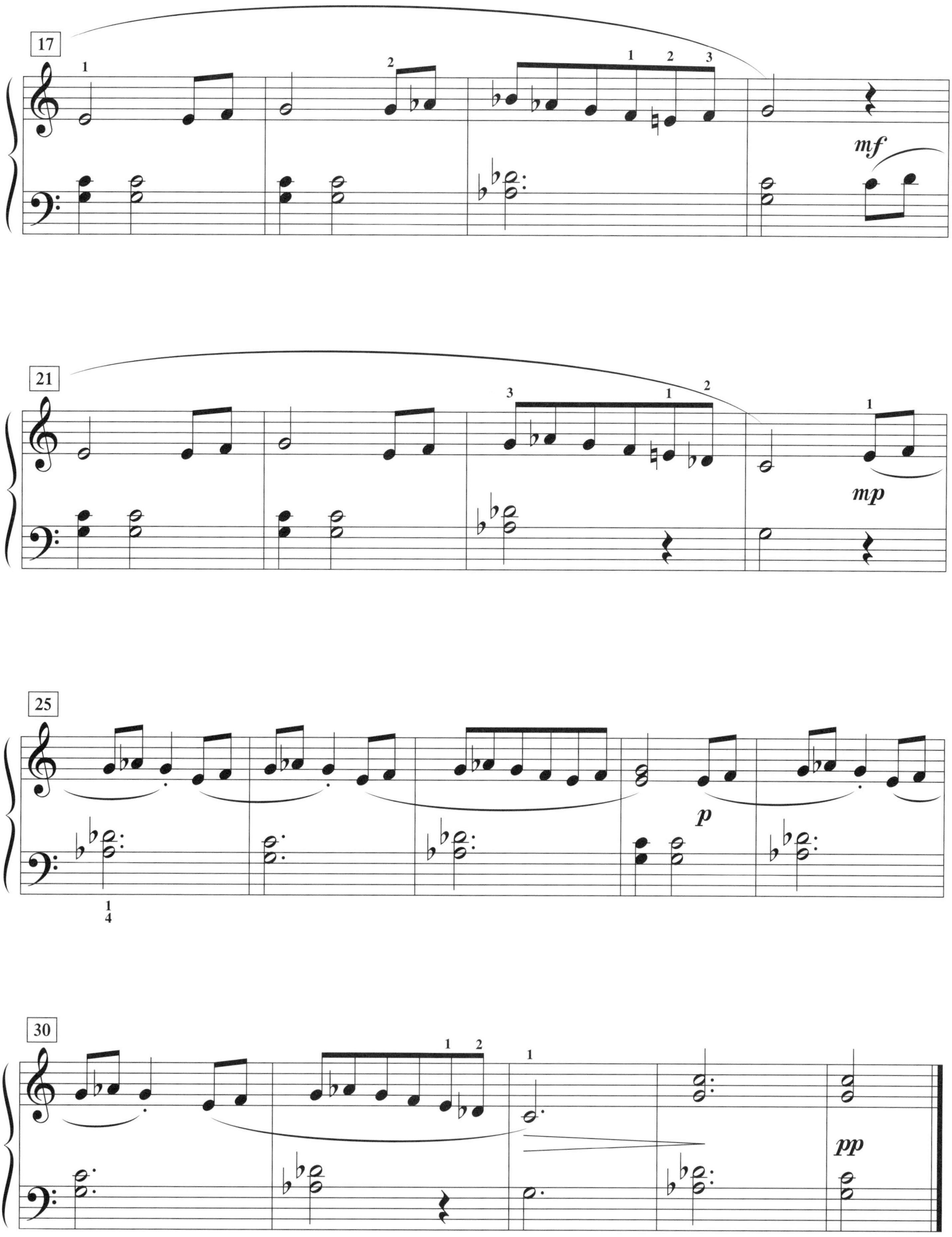

Fire Dance

Secondo

Timothy Brown

With energy! (♩= ca. 160)

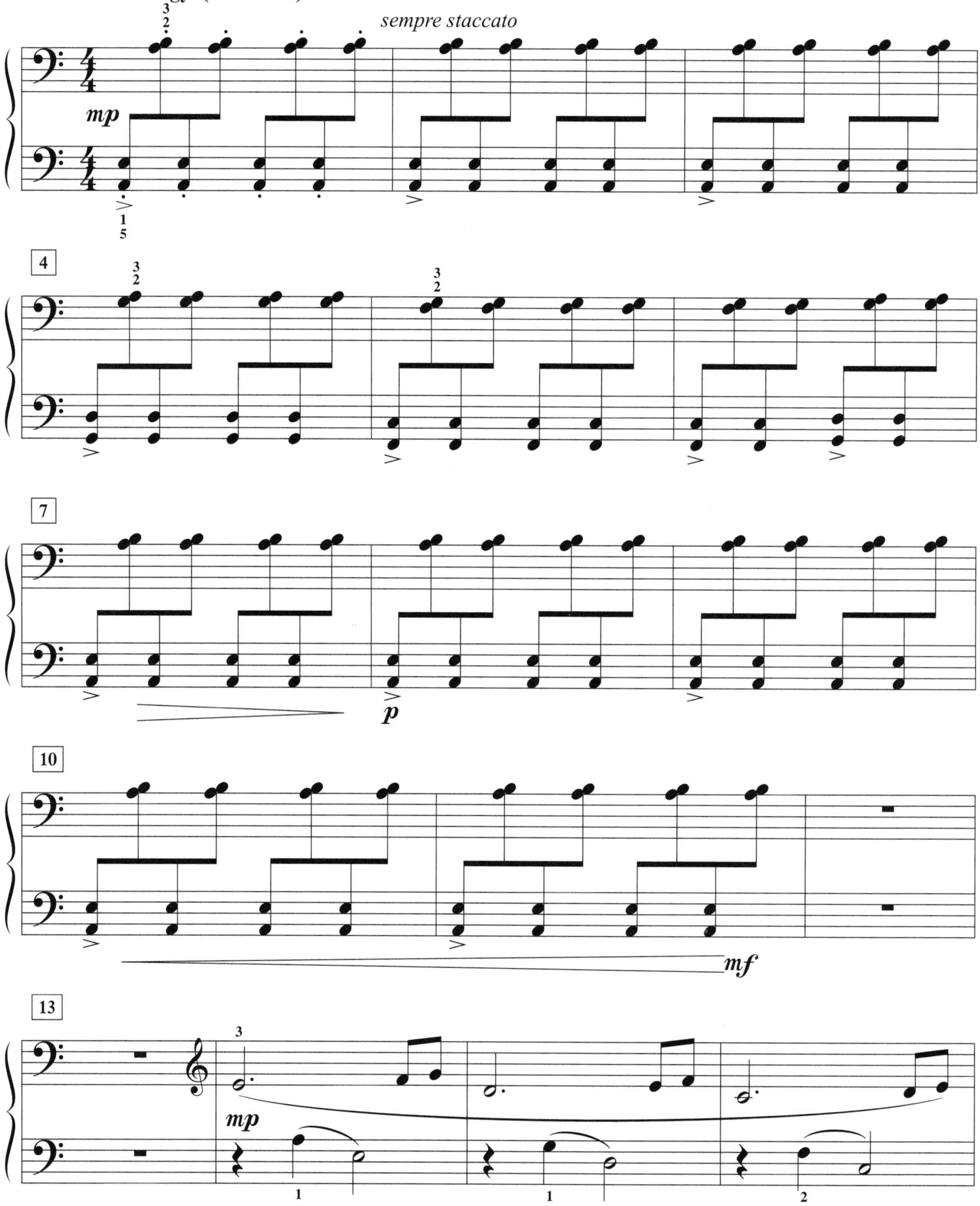

Fire Dance

Primo

Timothy Brown

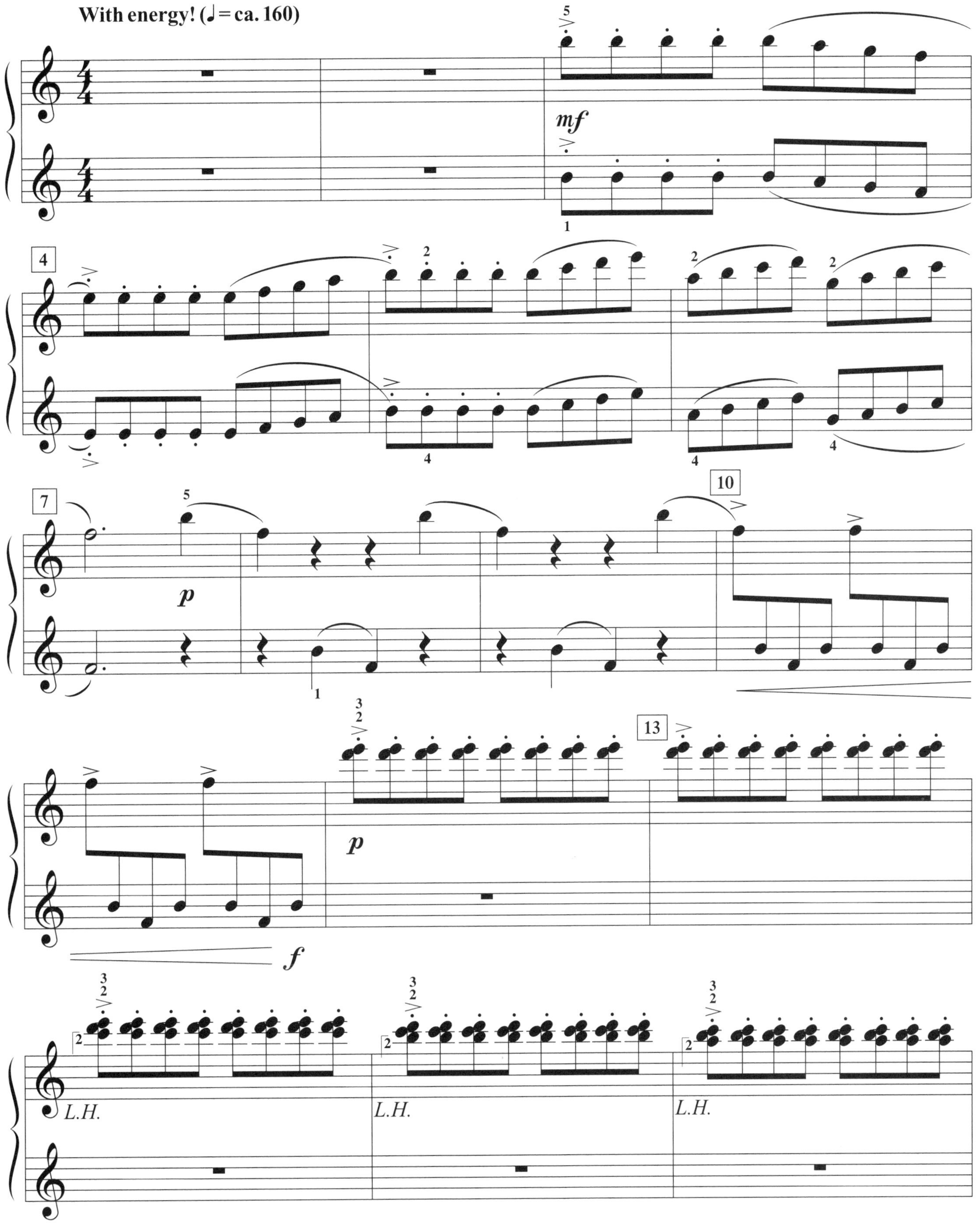

Secondo

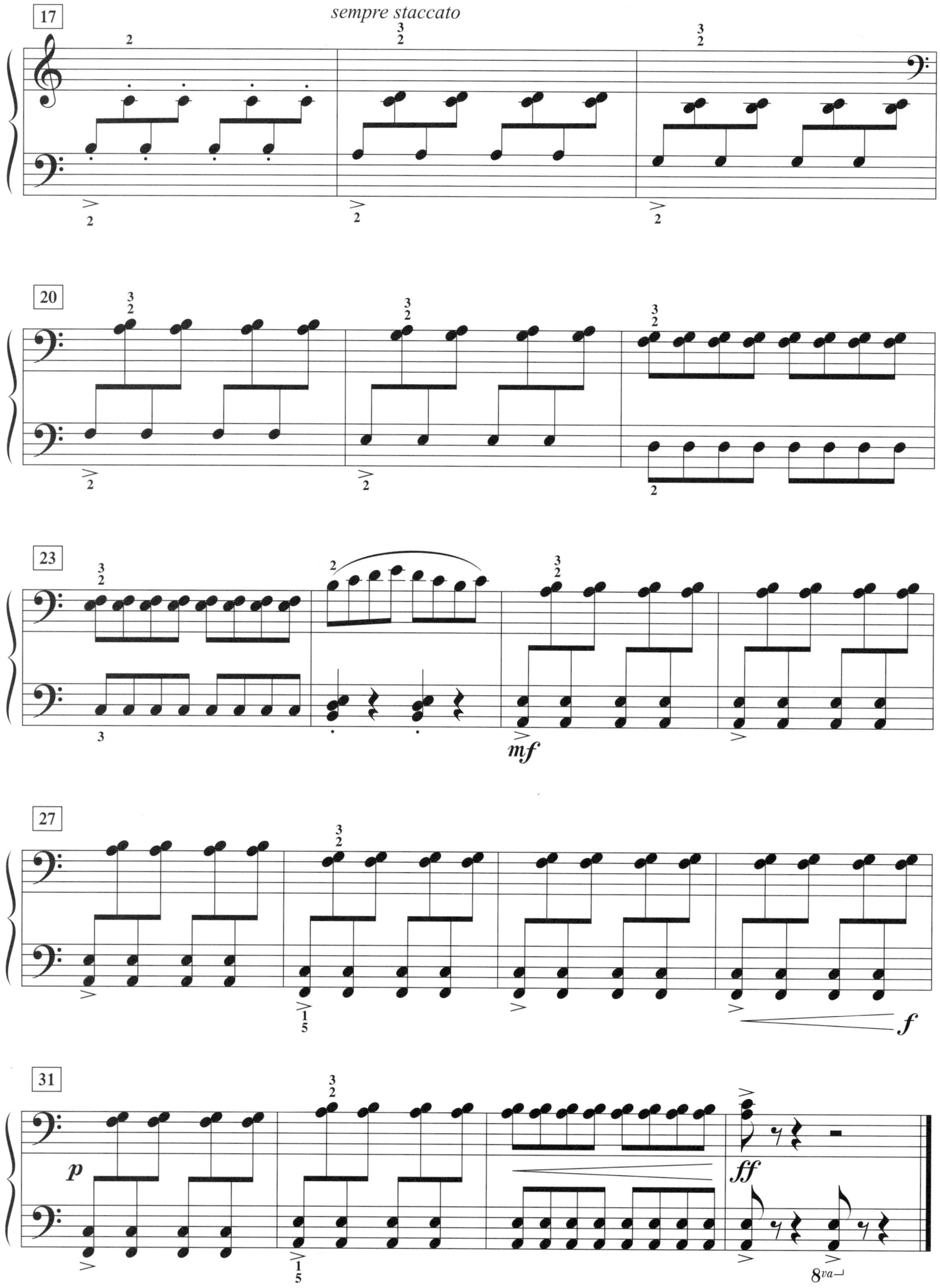

Primo

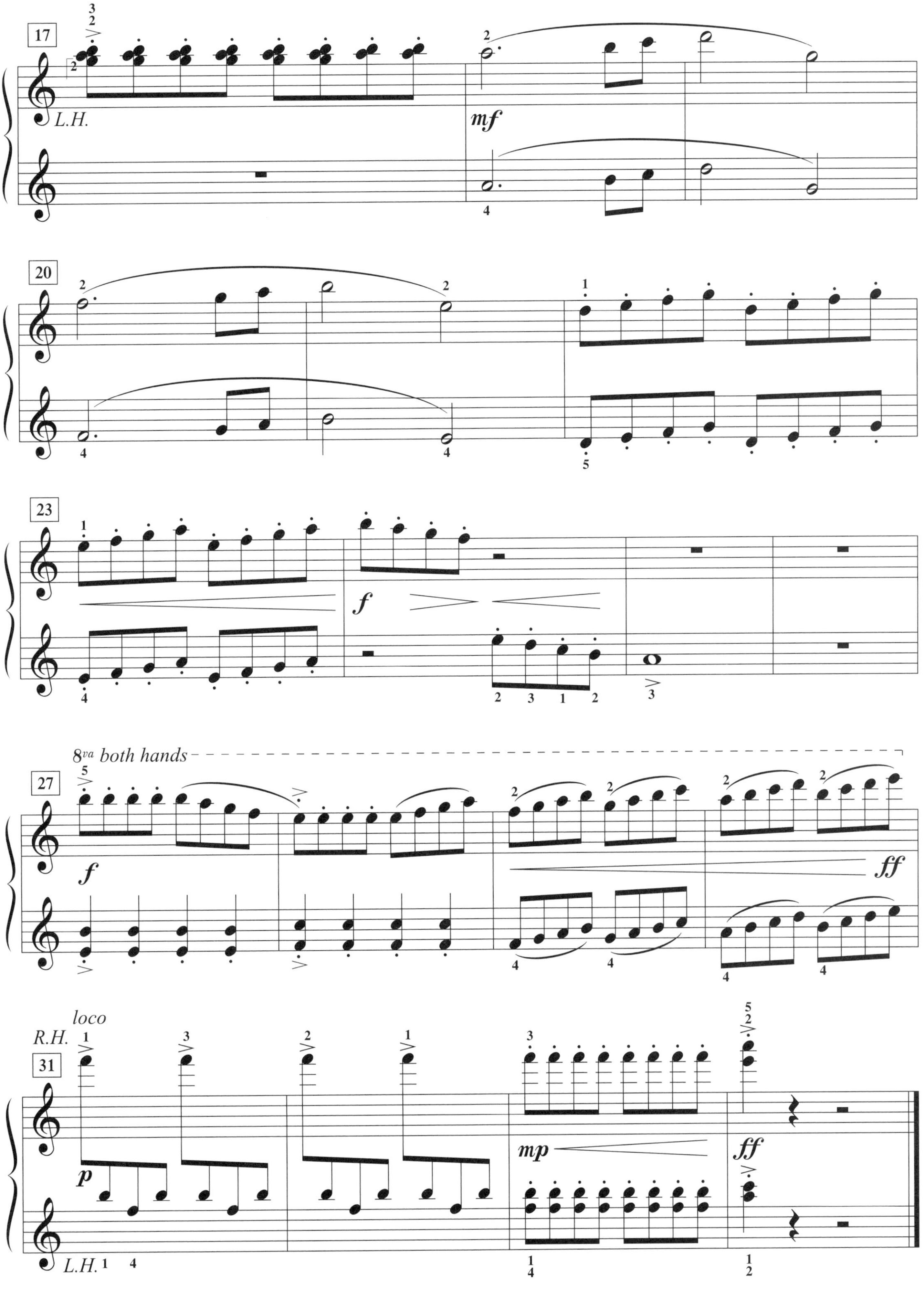

About the Arrangers

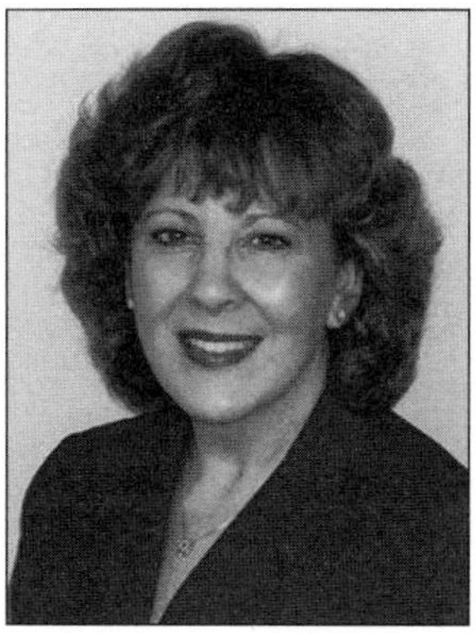

Melody Bober

Piano instructor, music teacher, composer, clinician—Melody Bober has been active in music education for over 25 years. As a composer, her goal is to create exciting and challenging pieces that are strong teaching tools to promote a lifelong love, understanding, and appreciation for music. Pedagogy, ear training, and musical expression are fundamentals of Melody's teaching, as well as fostering composition skills in her students.

Melody graduated with highest honors from the University of Illinois with a degree in music education, and later received a master's degree in piano performance. She maintains a large private studio, performs in numerous regional events, and conducts workshops across the country. She and her husband Jeff reside in Minnesota.

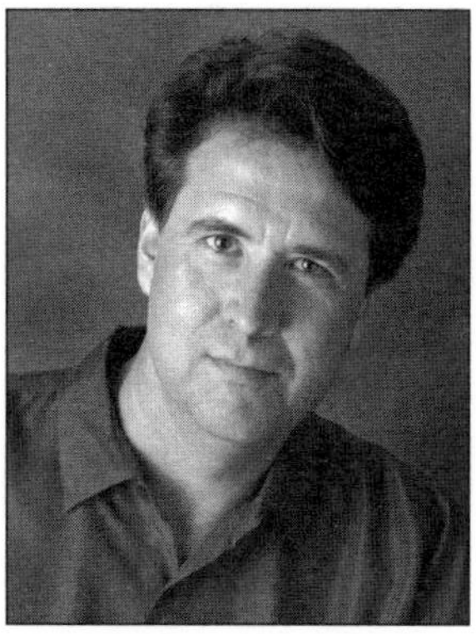

Timothy Brown

Timothy Brown holds a master's degree in piano performance from the University of North Texas, where he studied piano with Adam Wodnicki and music composition with Newel Kay Brown. He was later a recipient of a research fellowship from the Royal Holloway, University of London, where he performed postgraduate studies in music composition and orchestration, studying with English composer Brian Lock. His numerous credits as a composer include first prize at the Aliénor International Harpsichord Competition for his harpsichord solo *Suite Española* (Centaur Records). Mr. Brown leads a very active career as an exclusive composer and clinician for The FJH Music Company Inc.

Mr. Brown's works have been performed by concert artist Elaine Funaro on NPR, and most recently at the Spoleto Music Festival and the Library of Congress Concert Series in Washington D.C. His numerous commissions include a commission by Clavier Magazine for his piano solo *Once Upon a Time*, edited by Denes Agay. Mr. Brown is currently a fine arts specialist for the Dallas Public Schools and serves on the advisory board of the Booker T. Washington High School for the Performing and Visual Arts in Dallas, Texas.

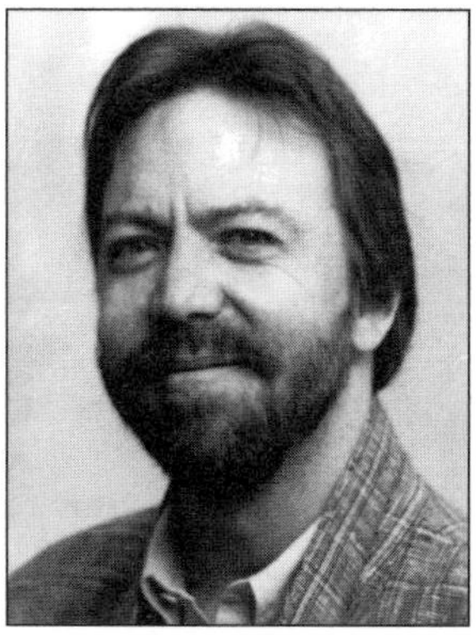

Edwin McLean

Edwin McLean is a freelance composer living in Chapel Hill, North Carolina. He is a graduate of the Yale School of Music, where he studied with Krzysztof Penderecki and Jacob Druckman. He also holds a master's degree in music theory and a bachelor's degree in piano performance from the University of Colorado.

Mr. McLean has been the recipient of several grants and awards: The MacDowell Colony, the John Work Award, the Woods Chandler Prize (Yale), Meet the Composer, Florida Arts Council, and many others. He has also won the Aliénor Composition Competition for his work *Sonata for Harpsichord*, published by The FJH Music Company Inc. and recorded by Elaine Funaro (*Into the Millennium*, Gasparo GSCD-331).

Since 1979, Edwin McLean has arranged the music of some of today's best known recording artists. Currently, he is senior editor as well as MIDI orchestrator for The FJH Music Company Inc.

About the Arrangers

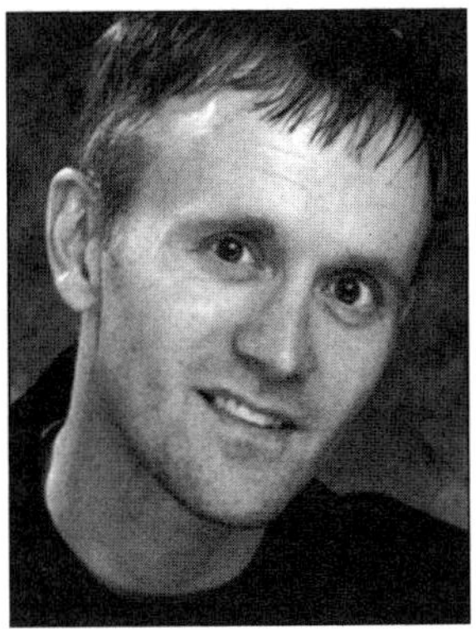

Kevin Olson

Kevin Olson is an active pianist, composer, and faculty member at Elmhurst College near Chicago, Illinois, where he teaches classical and jazz piano, music theory, and electronic music. He holds a Doctor of Education degree from National-Louis University, and bachelor's and master's degrees in music composition and theory from Brigham Young University. Before teaching at Elmhurst College, he held a visiting professor position at Humboldt State University in California.

A native of Utah, Kevin began composing at the age of five. When he was twelve, his composition *An American Trainride* received the Overall First Prize at the 1983 National PTA Convention in Albuquerque, New Mexico. Since then, he has been a composer-in-residence at the National Conference on Piano Pedagogy and has written music for the American Piano Quartet, Chicago a cappella, the Rich Matteson Jazz Festival, and several piano teachers associations around the country.

Kevin maintains a large piano studio, teaching students of a variety of ages and abilities. Many of the needs of his own piano students have inspired a diverse collection of books and solos published by The FJH Music Company Inc., which he joined as a writer in 1994.

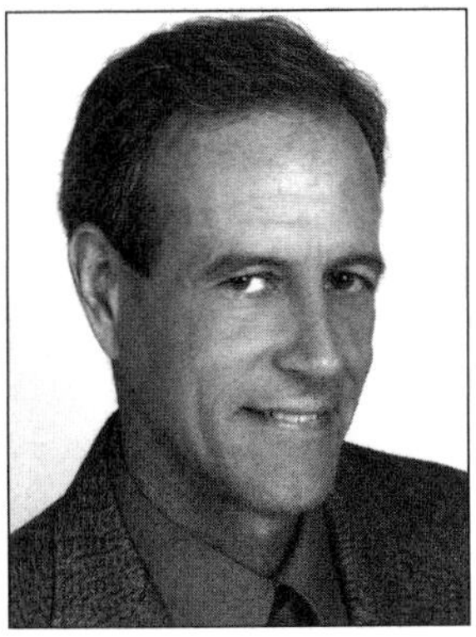

Robert Schultz

Robert Schultz, composer, arranger, and editor, has achieved international fame during his career in the music publishing industry. The Schultz Piano Library, established in 1980, has included more than 500 publications of classical works, popular arrangements, and Schultz's original compositions in editions for pianists of every level from the beginner through the concert artist. In addition to his extensive library of published piano works, Schultz's output includes original orchestral works, chamber music, works for solo instruments, and vocal music.

Schultz has presented his published editions at workshops, clinics, and convention showcases throughout the United States and Canada. He is a long-standing member of ASCAP and has served as president of the Miami Music Teachers Association. Mr. Schultz's original piano compositions and transcriptions are featured on the compact disc recordings *Visions of Dunbar* and *Tina Faigen Plays Piano Transcriptions*, released on the ACA Digital label and available worldwide. His published original works for concert artists are noted in Maurice Hinson's *Guide to the Pianist's Repertoire, Third Edition*. He currently devotes his full time to composing and arranging, writing from his studio in Miami, Florida. In-depth information about Robert Schultz and The Schultz Piano Library is available at the Web site www.schultzmusic.com.

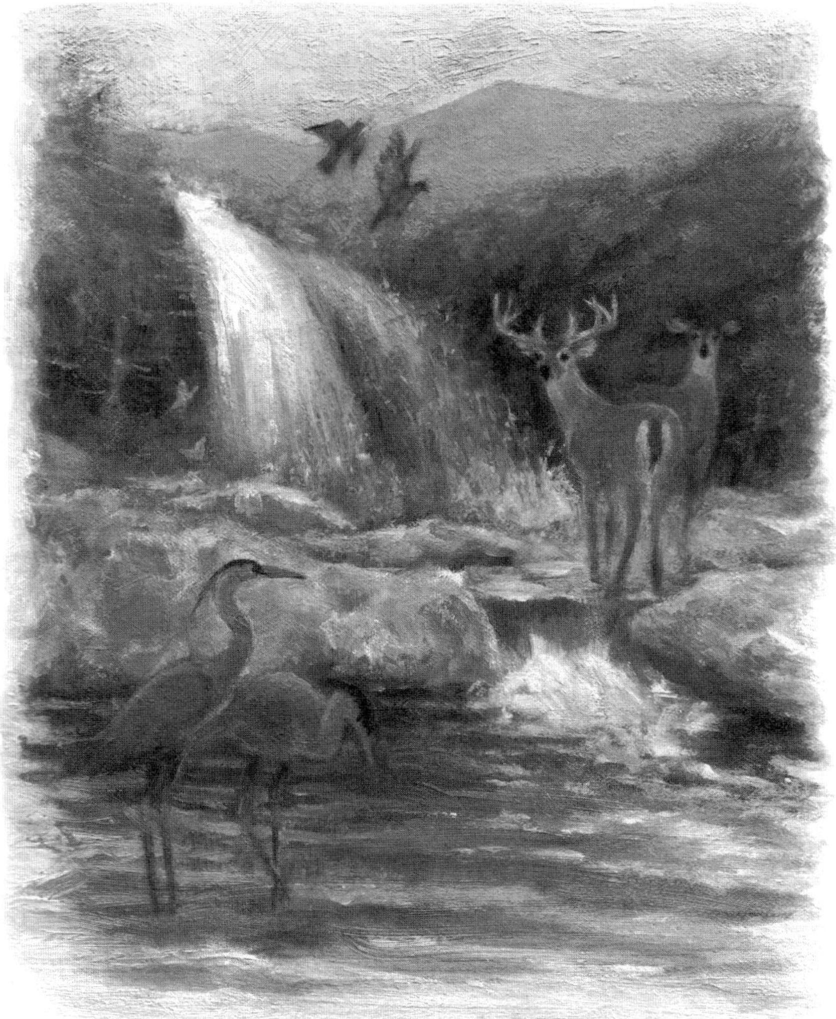